CREATIVITY
for CRITICAL
THINKERS

*Anthony Weston
and Byron Stoyles*

OXFORD
UNIVERSITY PRESS

OXFORD

UNIVERSITY PRESS

8 Sampson Mews, Suite 204, Don Mills, Ontario M3C 0H5
www.oupcanada.com

Oxford University Press is a department of the University of Oxford.
It furthers the University's objective of excellence in research, scholarship,
and education by publishing worldwide in

Oxford New York

Auckland Cape Town Dar es Salaam Hong Kong Karachi
Kuala Lumpur Madrid Melbourne Mexico City Nairobi
New Delhi Shanghai Taipei Toronto

With offices in

Argentina Austria Brazil Chile Czech Republic France Greece
Guatemala Hungary Italy Japan Poland Portugal Singapore
South Korea Switzerland Thailand Turkey Ukraine Vietnam

Oxford is a trade mark of Oxford University Press
in the UK and in certain other countries

Published in Canada
by Oxford University Press

Library and Archives Canada Cataloguing in Publication

Weston, Anthony, 1954–
Creativity for critical thinkers / Anthony Weston & Byron Stoyles.—
1st Canadian ed.

Includes bibliographical references.
ISBN 978-0-19-543251-0

1. Creative ability. 2. Critical thinking. I. Stoyles, Byron J.
(Byron James), 1975- II. Title.

BF408.W48 2010   153.3'5   C2010-900349-7

Cover image: Matthew Hertel/iStockphoto

Oxford University Press is committed to our environment. This book is printed on
Forest Stewardship Council certified paper, harvested from a responsibly managed forest.

Mixed Sources
Product group from well-managed
forests and other controlled sources
www.fsc.org Cert no. SW-COC-000952
© 1996 Forest Stewardship Council

Printed and bound in Canada

1 2 3 4 – 13 12 11 10

CONTENTS

Creative thinking generates new ideas and new ways of organizing existing ideas. Creativity is the ability that allows us to expand possibility—to find unexpected movement in problems that have us stumped. It is, to use a popular phrase, the ability to think 'outside of the box'.

While some people seem naturally predisposed to thinking creatively, most of us need to work to at it. Creativity can be learned. Creativity for Critical Thinkers provides the basic tools for developing your creativity.

This book is designed to provide a short, simple, and engaging introduction to creative thinking. It is specifically aimed at teaching creativity to *critical thinkers*. 'Critical thinking' usually focuses on the identification and evaluation of arguments. These are important skills and are widely taught. Yet, even the most specific argument must be evaluated partly against the background of what else is possible. The methods taught in this book provide ways of understanding how the world *could be* and this gives us a whole new view of how the world *is*.

Of course, critical thinking is not restricted to *criticism*. True, we usually practice our critical thinking skills by evaluating other people's arguments. This serves another purpose, however: understanding what makes a good argument is also necessary for generating original, and compelling, new arguments. Critical thinking can help us *identify the need* for new ideas. It is not, however, well-suited to generating these new ideas. For this, creativity, not criticism, is required. The methods introduced in this book provide the means to generate new ideas. These methods are easy to learn and effective in practice.

For general readers, this book is an engaging introduction to creative thinking. The methods introduced in the book stand on their own. No prior knowledge on the part of the reader is assumed. *Creativity for Critical Thinkers* is, however, primarily designed to supplement texts for college- and university-level courses in critical thinking. Most critical thinking texts overlook or neglect methods for creative thinking as an aspect of practical reasoning. This book fills the void resulting from this tendency. *Creativity for Critical Thinkers* is not intended to carry a class by itself—for the more familiar argument-analysis and logical skills you will have to look elsewhere—but it will add an indispensable and sometimes exciting element.

Instructors interested in using this book as a supplementary text will find suggestions in the 'Notes for Instructors' section following the preface. The notes include suggestions for evaluating students' skills in creative thinking.

In adapting this book for a Canadian audience, I have worked to retain the spirit of Anthony Weston's original text. Weston's style of writing is informal, even conversational. While the informal prose is atypical for a university- or college-level text, this is actually one of the book's strengths. Not only is *Creativity for Critical Thinkers* easy to read, but it conveys Weston's enthusiasm for creative thinking. This enthusiasm is infectious—one cannot help but feel that no problem is too big for the methods outlined in this book.

For the most part, changes to Weston's original text have been introduced only as required to better clarify specific ideas, to make the 'For Practice' exercises more user-friendly for instructors, and to give the book a distinctly Canadian flavour.

I am thankful for the support and guidance of the editorial staff at OUP Canada, especially Ryan Chynces, Jodi Lewchuk, Mark Thompson, and Dana Hopkins. I am also thankful for the constructive feedback provided by those who reviewed the complete manuscript. I am always thankful for the support of my colleagues at Trent University and, especially, for the support of my family.

I welcome insightful comments, constructive criticisms, and creative suggestions.

Byron Stoyles
Peterborough, Ontario
byronstoyles@trentu.ca

Notes For Instructors

Courses in critical thinking are generally designed to introduce students to various techniques related to thinking rationally. These courses frequently include the basics of formal logic—especially propositional logic—though this is not the only topic covered. In teaching critical thinking, we also teach students how to identify and avoid common fallacies, and we teach students how to assess inductive arguments.

The myriad examples of 'real-life' arguments scattered throughout textbooks designed for use in critical thinking courses make clear that the methods of reasoning being presented are supposed to be practical. Critical thinking, however, is only one aspect of 'practical reasoning' or 'practical thinking'.

Recognizing patterns of reasoning allows us to identify and assess arguments. Understanding the structure of deductively valid and inductively cogent arguments is also a first step to generating strong arguments of our own. It is, however, only one step. Original, and compelling, arguments rarely result from the mere insertion of claims into the structure of a valid argument. (Though *modus ponens* is always a valid form, not all arguments with this form are compelling—or even interesting for that matter.) Creativity is needed too.

The methods introduced in this book are meant to supplement, rather than compete with, the skills typically developed in critical thinking courses. Thus, the content can be incorporated into existing sections of a course—for instance, in a section devoted to generating original arguments.

Introducing the methods of creative thinking included in *Creativity for Critical Thinkers* is one way to help open students' minds to new possibilities and new ways of seeing the world. Since the book invites students to recognize what is *possible*, the content can also be used to help students reflect on their own assumptions and the assumptions of others. This is especially helpful when evaluating historical arguments in context.

Students who are new to philosophy are sometimes frustrated by philosophers' willingness to call into question ideas that aren't normally challenged. Students who are able to think creatively are more likely to recognize that 'the way things have always been' is not always the way things must, or should, be. If students are introduced even to some of the methods of creative thinking presented here—especially in Chapters 1–3—they will start thinking in new ways. These methods can help students to see the difference between what is necessary and what is contingent. Thus, creative thinking can be an asset for students by helping them to understand the basics of modal reasoning without the need for introducing technical jargon. Even on a surface level, these skills are useful for assessing the acceptability and truth of premises in arguments.

You might consider using the methods introduced in *Creativity for Critical Thinkers* as a means for helping students better understand aspects of inductive or non-deductive reasoning. Inferences to the best explanation, for example, are often the result of creative thinking. The clever sleuth is the one who, by thinking creatively, generates the explanation that we (reasonably) infer must be true because it is the best available explanation for the facts of her case. It takes creativity to generate explanations for empirical facts. Evaluating inferences to the best explanation is easier when students are able to identify explanations other than the one being considered. This too requires creativity.

Students often assume that causal reasoning of the sort employed in scientific/empirical reasoning is the best example of purely rational, objective, reasoning. Yet, on the received view, there is no formula for generating hypotheses or theories: scientific discoveries tend to be serendipitous or the result of creative thought. What's more, the 'confirmation' of a scientific theory remains a matter of inductive reasoning. Thus, there are opportunities for incorporating the content of this book if your course includes a unit on empirical or causal reasoning.

Creativity for Creative Thinkers can also be used to develop an independent section of a course—a section devoted entirely to the creative side of practical reasoning.

Though this text includes some comments regarding the ways in which creative thinking is related to critical thinking, and certain exercises in the 'For Practice' sections point to this relation, the text focuses almost exclusively on presenting methods for creative thinking. The focus on methods for creative thinking allows you more flexibility for incorporating the content of this book into your course. Because the material in *Creativity for Critical Thinkers* complements, but doesn't overlap, the content of texts devoted to critical thinking, it is well suited to supplement most critical thinking texts.

Because the book is short and the style casual, college and university students will be able to work through it at a rapid pace. What's more, the book invites self-directed study and is intended to be self-explanatory. Thus, class time can be devoted to fine-tuning the methods introduced and, more importantly, to practicing these methods. The 'For Practice' exercises at the end of each chapter provide students with opportunities to improve their skills. Additional exercises are easy to generate—indeed, students can be asked to start each session by identifying additional problems.

There are many ways to evaluate students' use of the methods introduced in this book. Here are a few:

Some courses reserve a portion of the final grade to reflect students' participation. In these courses, part of the participation grade could be assigned to reflect students' participation in discussions and activities tied to creative thinking. One option is to award participations points for completing exercises assigned from the 'For Practice' section at the end of each chapter—regardless of the quality of the ideas generated. Another is to award participation points for working in small groups to generate possible solutions to specific problems. These can be problems identified in the book or other problems of interest to the students.

Evaluating students' work in these ways makes it possible to use objective standards insofar as the quantity of work is being assessed rather than the quality. This is appropriate for the reason that some of the methods introduced in this book are built on the assumption that we will eventually generate good ideas if we generate many ideas.

Alternatively, creative thinking could be incorporated into a bigger project. Students could be required to present their ideas in a (formal) debate or they could be required to write a position paper on an assigned topic. Both of these alternatives allow opportunities for combining creative thinking with the skills typically taught in critical thinking courses. Students can be encouraged to generate an original argument according to the principles of good reasoning rather than simply analyzing others' arguments. Position papers containing original arguments can be assessed using the methods familiar to most instructors. You might, in this case, earmark a portion of the grade for the originality of the students' ideas.

Another possibility, appropriate for courses with students who are interested in business, is to assign the students the task of developing a new product or service using the methods in the book. For evaluation, students might submit a basic business plan. Or perhaps better, students could submit a summary of the creative process that lead to their plan—the summary could indicate which methods they used to generate an original product or service and which methods they used to build on their breakthrough idea. (This sort of project is typical in business and pre-business programs. Students in these programs have generated quite promising ideas in the past. For example, one such idea formed the basis of what is now *FedEx*.)

Courses designed to incorporate quizzes, tests, or exams can build in questions requiring students to identify or explain the various ideas and methods introduced here.

When introducing the methods of creative thinking it is important to encourage students to give each method a chance. In the original edition of this book, Weston warns that teachers unfamiliar with this material should take a bit of care to convey a positive attitude. It is important to give each idea enough time to work (especially ideas generated by what seem, initially, to be improbable methods like exotic association). Among other things, this requires us to avoid the tendency to 'edit' or tone down students' ideas. Challenge students to expand their ideas. This may require some degree of prodding or even provocation. Once students get started, the results can be very rewarding.

Notes For Students

You have probably been told that the skills you learn in a critical thinking course are useful. This is true. The ability to identify and assess arguments is invaluable for understanding the views of other people and for reflecting on your own views.

What you probably haven't been told is that critical thinking is not, on its own, sufficient for addressing many real problems. For this, creativity is needed too. Creative thinking complements critical thinking—both are practical ways of thinking; both are useful.

Creativity for Critical Thinkers is designed to introduce you to methods of creative thinking. Creative thinking is a different aspect of practical reasoning than critical thinking, so you will find that there is little direct overlap between the content of this book and other texts the instructor has chosen for your course.

Despite the lack of direct overlap, there are many ways in which creative thinking can be related to the critical skills necessary for identifying and evaluating arguments. Thus, as you read this book, you are invited to consider how the methods of creative thinking are related to the methods of critical thinking you are learning in your course. How, exactly, do they complement one another?

For one thing, creative thinking opens your mind to new possibilities. This can be useful as we assess other people's arguments—a task in which we are often our own worst enemies. It is natural to find arguments compelling only if they support conclusions with which we already agree. We are quick to look for problems with arguments supporting conclusions that go against what we believe. Arguments, however, are meant to convince us of something that we might not otherwise accept, not simply to support what we already believe. As the saying goes, this would amount to 'preaching to the choir'.

In order to give each argument a fair assessment, it is important to keep an open mind. Unfortunately, keeping our minds open to different possibilities is often challenging. We can become set in our ways of seeing the world. (How often do you find yourself thinking, 'but that's not the way things are!' or 'it's always been that way!'?) Our challenge is to refrain from judging the strength of arguments before they have been properly evaluated using the tools you are learning in your critical thinking course.

Practicing the methods of creative thinking presented in this book can help—creative thinking generates new ideas and opens our minds to possibilities we may not otherwise see. With a little creativity, we come to recognize that almost everything could be different—and maybe even better.

The content of this book is meant to be practical. Rather than presenting you with endless data and theories, *Creativity for Critical Thinkers* presents methods that you can try right away. You will likely find that these methods are easy to use. Indeed, you might find that some of the methods introduced in this book are so easy, they at first seem a bit silly or implausible. Nevertheless, it is important to give each method a chance, because they have been selected for a reason: they work.

Even the most creative people can become more creative with practice. As you read this book, you may find that practice is especially helpful for realizing exactly how a method is supposed to work. It's one thing to read examples of creative thinking. It's quite another to use these methods to generate your own solutions to real problems. To get started, you are encouraged to take advantage of the 'For Practice' assignments at the end of each chapter even if these are not assigned by your instructor.

Unlike some textbooks, *Creativity for Critical Thinkers* isn't overburdened with technical language or jargon. The text is designed to present ideas in an accessible and engaging way. Likely, you will find yourself working through the text at a fast pace. You might even find that you enjoy it.

Creative thinking is not something that stops at a certain point as though it were a finish line. With this in mind, none of the creative solutions presented in this book are 'final answers'. The examples are not necessarily the best solutions to the problems being considered. In some cases, you might not even think they are overly good solutions. If you find yourself thinking that you have better ideas, use the methods in this book to build on them. Indeed, you *should* challenge yourself to think of better ideas than the ones presented in the book. When you succeed, the book's purpose will be served.

CHAPTER ONE

CREATIVITY'S PROMISE

AT THE BUS STOP

You are driving along in your sporty little two-seater. It is cold and raining. You come to a bus stop, where three people are waiting for the bus. One is a stranger, who keels over with a heart attack just as you pull up. Next is an old friend who once saved your life. The last, believe it or not, is the man or woman of your dreams. What do you do?

At first glance there is no single good answer. The stranger clearly needs to get to a hospital as quickly as possible. Your old friend could also use a ride, and you certainly owe her. But then there is the man or woman of your dreams, whom otherwise you may never see again. And you have only one seat in your car . . .

So how creative are you? Think about it for a moment before reading on. What would you do?

This little brainteaser was used on a real job application as a test of creativity.[1] As the tale goes, the winning job candidate didn't hesitate before giving his answer: 'I would give the car keys to my old friend and ask her to take the stranger to the hospital on her way home, and then I would stay behind and wait for the bus with the woman of my dreams'.

Think about this answer. If you're like most people, you approached the problem by mentally reviewing your options. And the way your mind shaped this mental review was to imagine taking each of the three people in your car in turn. 'I could take the stranger, but then. . .' 'I could take the man or woman of my dreams, but then. . .' What most people do *not* do is ask themselves if there are any options *besides offering one of the three people a ride*. Ask this question, though, and you are immediately 'thinking outside of the box'—and when you do that, coming up with a great answer becomes easy.

What this story shows is that 'thinking outside of the box' is not hard to learn. All you have to do is learn to ask the question: 'What about *other* options?'

There is another point as well. *Even situations in which you seem totally 'stuck' have unsuspected possibilities.*

Many people who pride themselves on being 'practical' might look at this situation and declare, 'Well, you just have to decide! Obviously there are three and only three possibilities. Just decide and get on with it!' But this is bad advice. '*Obviously* there are three and only three possibilities'? As the great fictional sleuth Sherlock Holmes once said, what's obvious isn't always true. There *are* other possibilities. What is really practical is to start looking for them.

Clarifying Your Problem

In many cases, it helps to approach your creative challenge with some analytical thinking up front. Start by carefully defining the problem. Being clear on the precise nature of the problem you face will better allow you to identify solutions. Defining the problem itself can be a creative act.

New possibilities open up as soon as you realize that the problem you face isn't to give one person a ride and leave the others behind. In this case, you feel some pull to help the dying stranger, or to repay your debt, but you also want to spend time with the man or woman of your dreams. The problem, then, is that it is not immediately obvious how to do more than one of these things using your two-seater car.

After you have clarified the problem, identify the elements of the perfect solution. *Then* start looking for specific new ideas. A perfect solution to the two-seater problem involves giving the heart attack victim a chance to live, while *simultaneously* honouring a debt to the old friend who saved your life *and* spending time with the man or woman

KEY POINTS

Creative thinking is the process of generating new ideas and new ways of organizing existing ideas. *Creativity* is the ability that allows us to cast a problem in a new light, which allows us to see possible solutions that were not immediately evident.

- Creative people are *critical*: they don't stop with the 'given' and the (supposedly) 'obvious'.
- Creative people are *imaginative*: they make a habit of thinking in open and elastic ways.
- Creative people are *inventive*: they consciously seek to devise new ideas and new ways of thinking.

of your dreams. A tall order? Sure, but not as difficult as giving three people a ride in one seat!

A ROCKY START

Consider now a scenario in a professional setting. You're an architect supervising the excavation for a building to be used as the research headquarters for a group of natural scientists. In keeping with the group's values, the original plan is to construct the first three floors of the four-story building below ground in order to minimize its visual and environmental impact. Shortly after the backhoe starts digging, it hits an enormous rock—harder to move than the walls of the structure you're about to build. What do you do?[2] You could give up; that's life, right? Or, you could look for a creative solution.

Maybe, after a big investment in bulldozers or explosives, you can make the hole you need—maybe with the extra ammunition it's now so big that you have to spend more time filling part of it back in with fragments of the rock you've just blown to bits.

Before leaping in with the dynamite, perhaps it is wise to look for other, more creative, solutions. To do this, one useful question to ask is, 'Are there better ways to get rid of the rock?' Maybe, with a bit more digging, you could locate preexisting cracks and use these to break the rock into pieces. Maybe you could rig up your backhoe with pulleys and winch it out. Or maybe, getting a *little* more creative, you could dig an even deeper hole and roll it in.

There's a little space in this. Basically, though, it's more of the same— like asking which of the three people at the bus stop you should take in your car. **Try instead for a better question.**

We've been asking, 'How do we move the rock?' But now, suppose we ask, 'Are there ways to get around this problem *without* moving the rock?'

New possibilities emerge the minute we ask this new question. One is to move the *building*—build it away from the rock. Must the building be right there? A little adjustment in your plans and there would be no problem.

Notice again that this is a different kind of question than the original. Maybe dynamite would be the best way to get rid of the rock—but maybe getting rid of the rock is not the best way to get rid of the *problem*. We need a little more mental flexibility in place of the straight-ahead mentality that simply perceives a problem, defines it in only one way, and charges ahead (and calls itself 'practical'!). Problem-solving expert Edward de Bono instead advocates what he calls 'lateral thinking'.[3] When you begin to imagine moving the whole building, you have stepped back from the immediate situation and begun to explore ways to sidestep the problem entirely.

Is there another step you might take with this problem too? Suppose you ask whether this rock is really a problem at all. Could there be a way to use this unexpected obstacle to your advantage? At first, this may seem totally improbable, even senseless. 'How is the rock not a problem? There is a rock right where we want the first floor of our building! Headquarters or rock, something's got to give!' But does it really?

If this rock first seems as immovable as a wall in the completed building, why not suppose it *were* a wall? How about building the structure around the rock? A really creative architect might seek permission to redesign the building itself, maybe making the rock a

CASE IN POINT

Arthur Erickson, an Albertan who trained as an architect at McGill University, was hired to design the University of Lethbridge campus. The building site posed serious challenges as it was made up of a flat plateau through which a deep valley was cut by the eroding forces of a river. One obvious tactic would be to avoid the challenges of building in and around a valley by designing the campus to sit on the plateau—away from the river and its eroding forces. This is the equivalent of moving the headquarters to avoid the rock. In this case, however, building away from the 'rock' would move the building away from the natural beauty of the valley itself.

Erickson's solution was to incorporate the design into the landscape. As a result of this creative approach, U of L's University Hall spans the river valley. Thus, it takes advantage of the beauty of the valley to inspire generations of scholars. Erickson's creative designs can also be found at Simon Fraser University and the University of British Columbia.[4]

natural feature in a meeting space, or using the rock as a naturally fire-resistant backdrop for a low-emissions wood-stove. With this, the headquarters could be far more dramatic and intriguing, not to mention less expensive, than it would have been otherwise. The rock is put to use, and what an appropriate use for a group concerned with the environment! Neither building nor rock moves, no dynamite is required, and the headquarters ends up with a truly unique feature for less money . . . where's the problem?

THE FIRST STEP TOWARD CREATIVITY IS TO CHANGE OUR VERY IDEA OF A 'PROBLEM'

Typically, the term 'problem' has negative overtones. Problems are to be avoided, regretted, or dealt with as quickly as possible. The temptation is to find the first workable answer and stop. Who, we might ask, wants to have problems? It might surprise you, but *we should learn to welcome problems.*

We should welcome problems as challenges to be met, occasions for ongoing thinking, and invitations to be imaginative. From this point of view we should not only welcome problems, we should seek them out. Problems provide nothing less than *opportunities to change the world.*

Notice that in this way we are invited to rethink critically our problems themselves. In the architect's case, real creativity begins not by finding ways to move the rock, but at the next step: thinking of moving or changing the *building.* You are no longer addressing the 'given' problem at all. Using the rock as a feature of the building is not a solution to anything like what we first thought of as 'the' problem. With some creativity you can *transform* the given problem—not merely into another problem, useful as that often might be, but into a genuine opportunity instead.

Think of our usual dislike of problems as a kind of *push.* We have a difficulty that makes us uncomfortable, which motivates us (however reluctantly and without much confidence) to remove the discomfort. Thinking this way, we just want to get past the problem, so any old Band-Aid solution will probably do. Recognize the space for creative transformation, however, and motivation works from the other direction. Now we are *pulled* toward something better. A Band-Aid fix is no longer enough. We're not interested in just papering over the problem and going back to sleep. As hokey as it sounds, we might even say we are inspired.

Moreover, as we shall soon see, this is true even of problems on the largest scale. There are creative opportunities in everything from the smallest everyday annoyance to the largest social issues. You can even make a well-paid career out of tackling them creatively. Unexpected and wonderful possibilities are there for the finding. But, of course, we need to *look* for them first!

SUMMARY

In this chapter, you are encouraged to realize creativity's promise. Developing your ability to think creatively takes effort. It can also be fun.
- Be Inventive. Start by clarifying what appears to be the problem, and then work to cast the problem in a new light.
- Be Imaginative. Keep your mind open and consider all unexplored possibilities, even those which first appear silly.
- Be Critical. Go beyond the 'given' and the 'obvious'. This allows you to think 'outside the box'.

FOR PRACTICE

1. Answer each of the following questions in order to identify the need and value of creative thinking:
   a) What are your own associations with the word 'problem'? What other words could be used to describe what we call 'problems'?
   b) Think of specific problems you've had. How have you dealt with these problems? Are there ways you'd like to improve how you respond to problems?
   c) Are there aspects of your own life you would like to improve? Imagining that anything is possible, in what ways could you improve these aspects of your life?
   d) In what ways could other people (political leaders, say, or teachers, taxi drivers, orthodontists, burglars . . .) use creativity too?

e) Identify one person you know who is creative. What sorts of things does he or she do (and others don't) that make him or her creative? To answer this question, you might talk to the person and ask how he or she does it.

2. All sorts of problems—personal, social, scientific, and philosophical—can be approached creatively. You will be asked to think about a variety of practical problems as you work through this book. To warm up, answer each of the following questions. Play with these; generate truly 'wild' answers to get a sense of the space creative thinking can open in each of the problems identified.

a) Can you identify improvements to the way we elect members of federal parliament?

b) Have all possible political systems already been invented? Can you imagine something truly new?

c) Have all possible forms of art been invented? (Think of the recent emergence of digital art, computer music, whale song, highly developed graffiti styles, art using wholly recycled materials or 're-art', etc.) What else is possible?

d) How do you think we might reduce the impact of waste-disposal on the environment? Are there alternatives to the usual proposals for cutting back on waste?

e) What if time travel were possible? What totally new opportunities might arise?

f) If you could genetically engineer human beings, what changes would you make? For example, would it be a good option to create photosynthetic humans (like plants, absorbing energy directly from the sun) so we wouldn't need to eat for energy?

3. Usually, we are invited to consider two explanations for the origin of the universe: that it was created intentionally in all its intricacy and scope by a Cosmic Architect or that an explosion caused the beginning (the 'Big Bang') and things evolved from there. How many different ways can you imagine that the universe might have come into being?

THE FORCE OF HABIT

According to Ronald Melzack, Professor Emeritus of Psychology at McGill University, it used to be almost impossible to get morphine—one of the most powerful painkillers—even if you were dying and in severe pain.[1] Primarily, doctors feared that morphine was addictive. Morphine is an opiate and was used for the wounded during the Civil War and again during World War I. Frequently, heavy use by wounded soldiers created serious problems, though many sources now report that, if properly used, morphine need not be addictive.

In any case, whether morphine is addictive hardly matters when people are already on their deathbeds. Somehow this little detail never quite registered, so for a whole generation, people died in unnecessary pain. The reason, it seems, was *habit*. Reacting to the addiction caused by the overuse of morphine in the past, doctors acquired a habit of avoidance. (It also didn't help that morphine is closely associated with other opiates—heroin, for one—so that the moral connotations associated with 'drug' also stuck in people's minds.)

So that's where we were: stuck. Strange as it now seems, the old habits and associations were not broken, even when (as we now see) they clearly did not apply. It hasn't escaped our notice either that death is a 'side effect' of large doses of morphine—something that may not matter to, and could even be welcomed by, someone who is in pain and dying already. For a long time, however, people literally could not see the absurdity of denying morphine to dying people. Habits became blinders. Lately we see more clearly on this issue—morphine is accepted, though still with reservations. Since careful administration has proven to safeguard against harm and addiction, morphine is used now to manage even the pain of patients who are not dying. This makes you wonder what other undetected absurdities are staring us in the face.

Psychologists have a word to describe these mental blinders, these habits, assumptions, and fixed ways of seeing: *set*. Set is a temporary state of readiness to respond to problems in a predetermined way. Set isn't always a bad thing. We can't figure everything out from the beginning every time—if this were required, we'd never get anything done. Most of the time we rely on our habits to get us through. And, for the most part, this is lucky for us. Can you imagine having to figure out how to put your shoes on each morning or how to brush your teeth each time your breath started to stink? Our habits can save us a lot of time and energy.

Unluckily for us, though, set also blocks *new* ways of seeing. It blocks flexibility and creativity. Sometimes the ruts of habit can be so deep that we can't see over the top of them, so to speak, which often means we can't even see that we're in them. And then we're really

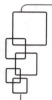

KEY POINTS

Researchers are aware of many ways in which we are blinded by assumptions, habits, and focus. When we focus on a specific task, for instance, we become blind to other things going on around us. One well-known experiment requires that subjects watch a video of people passing basketballs to one another and count the number of passes made. Partway through the video, a person in a gorilla costume dances around in the midst of the basketball action. Many subjects are so focused on counting the number of passes that they fail to notice the dancing gorilla—they simply do not see it. This phenomenon is known as *inattention blindness.*[2]

For another example, we are sometimes blinded by our assumptions about what is likely to occur. Most of us, for instance, assume that the concurrence of two events—say, a large meteorite hitting Earth *and* Earth spinning off its axis—is more likely than the occurrence of either one of these events on its own—a large meteorite hitting Earth *or* Earth spinning off its axis. Perhaps this is because we think the occurrence of one makes more likely the occurrence of the other—it is possible that a large meteorite could cause Earth to spin off its axis. Simple probability makes clear, however, that the opposite is true: it's far more likely that one of these events will occur than that both will occur. Yet, we don't see this. Experts call this the *conjunction problem.*[3]

These are but two of the many examples we have of the kinds of 'blinders' that get in the way of creative thinking. These phenomena make clear the need to challenge our assumptions and to keep an open mind—focusing on one problem or one aspect of a problem can blind us to other factors and possibilities.

stuck. We should welcome the opportunity to break set whenever we face a problem where our habitual responses are inappropriate *or* whenever we have a bit of free time to shake things up by trying something new.

THE NEED FOR A METHOD

We need *methods* to help us break set, or think outside the box. It's not enough for someone just to say 'Be creative!' or 'Break your habits!' Without any further help, we'll still just keep traveling around the same old circles and end up in pretty much the same place. Sitting with furrowed brows, tensing the mental muscles—the very image of Someone Thinking Really Hard—gets us nowhere.

To break out, we need to loosen up, to try something new. Be forewarned that thinking in new ways may feel somewhat forced. That's just the point: you're trying to entice yourself out beyond your own habits, out of the mental 'box' that confines you, beyond the familiar

KEY POINTS

We've all had a *eureka* moment: a moment when the answer, which had previously not occurred to us, seems suddenly obvious. (For an account of the eponymous eureka moment, see the story of Archimedes in Chapter 5.)

Though scientists haven't yet been able to explain just how we come to have eureka moments (*eureka* means 'I've found it' in Greek), they have discovered that different parts of the brain are active when answers come to us from 'out of the blue' than when we think through a problem systematically. Eureka moments are the result of subconscious brain processes that reorganize information related to the problems that have us stumped.

The research also indicates that, for a eureka moment, a relaxed and open mind is needed. The methods introduced in this book are designed to move us away from head-on approaches to solving problems. Creative thinking generates ideas. By generating ideas from random, and often wild, prompts we open our minds to new possibilities.[4]

world that is so comforting but that can also be so constraining. Boxes like these can be very strong. We need some equally forceful ways to shake things up, to see the world in a broader way.

Thinking outside the box requires adopting methods that may at first seem peculiar or improbable. So expect some methods that may feel unusual or awkward. You may be tempted not to take them seriously or use them only half-heartedly. Don't! They may seem silly, cumbersome, even embarrassing (to do in public, anyway); *but this is just what they need to be.* The whole point is to get out beyond your safety zone, the familiar ground that is also where you get 'stuck'. However silly they seem, the methods in this book are effective. Challenge yourself to play along, trust the process . . . take the leap.

Inviting Exotic Associations

This chapter introduces one method—just one—for thinking creatively. By looking at a single method, we can explore it in enough detail to get a good sense of how to use it and what it can do. You may find this simple method surprising, though it is in fact one of the most widely recommended methods by creativity experts.[5] It is recommended because it works.

The method is this. Start with a random prompt, then ask what new ideas or associations it provokes when put together with your problem. The prompt itself can come from literally *anywhere*: something you see or hear while walking down the street, chance words in a conversation, a film, a dictionary, a textbook, a mystery novel, a dream, a magazine, or wherever. If you are using words, usually it is best to have a source with a varied and rich vocabulary—find a good classic writer, maybe— but you can even find prompts on billboards along the highway or by turning on the radio for a few seconds. Even something as mundane as an accidental misspelling can sometimes suggest a new idea or a more vivid turn of phrase.

This method is called inviting 'exotic associations' or 'free associations'. The method works best if you start with a truly random, unusual, or 'exotic', source of associations. This will serve as a prompt—a new, unfiltered stimulus to your thinking—from outside your rut. Right away, we have something fresh!

A First Example

You've probably seen brain teasers asking you to think of some every-day object like a brick or a cheap ballpoint pen and imagine what else could be done with it. The challenge is to invent not just one or two new uses but lots of them; the challenge is to stretch your mind.

So let's try it with, say, *a burned-out light bulb.*

Pretty unpromising, right? On the face of it, you can't do anything with a burned-out light bulb at all except toss it in the trash. But now let's try to get creative.

With no method at all you might come up with a few new uses. You might, for example, paint the bulb and use it for a Christmas tree ornament. While old-school round bulbs could be made into traditional ball-shaped decorations, spiraled compact fluorescent bulbs would add a different touch. Extending this idea, flashlight bulbs might make nice earrings. Already, you have two ideas. But you need a lot more.

Try the exotic association method using random words as prompts. Here is an example of the thought process that might occur when using this method.

> *Amidst the debris on my desk right now I have Bill Bryson's book* In a Sunburned Country, *a rollicking Australian travelogue—certainly a random source for our problem. Opening it without looking, I just drop my finger onto the page and there is a word: 'cork-like'.*
>
> *That's certainly random! (As it happens, Bryson is writing about how his airplane seemed to pop out of the clouds one day.) At first it seems silly to start with this word, but I'll give it a try. Could there be possibilities even in this (literally) out-of-the-blue prompt?*
>
> *Hmm . . . could an old light bulb be made into some kind of bottle-stopper—that is, like a cork? Or what if it had a stopper—that is, if it were made into some sort of container itself? I let myself make free associations—one thing reminding me of something else that pops into my head. This reminds me of how, in some specialty stores, you see old wine bottles that have been cut in half to make a mug (the bottom) and a goblet (the top, turned upside down with a base added). So what about light bulbs? Of course, the glass is a lot thinner, but some glasses are made that way deliberately—it's classy.*

So how about making the light bulbs into champagne glasses? Their fragility could now be part of their appeal.

Notice already: this is a truly new idea, definitely 'outside of the box' compared to how we were thinking just a minute ago. And we didn't just mechanically 'apply' a random word (that is, champagne glasses aren't cork-like and they don't themselves have corks). Rather, the prompt did just what it was supposed to do: it *prompted* us along a different path—a *new* path. One free association opened up the field for others.

I pick another word at random from Bryson's book: 'battlefield'. Hmm . . . what about smashing the bulb and using the base, with its remaining jagged edges, as a weapon? Since there are light bulbs nearly everywhere and any kind of bulb will do, you can almost always make yourself a weapon in a pinch.

A third randomly selected word is 'likeable'. If we can paint a bulb as a Christmas ornament, why not paint the bulb red and send it to someone I like as a valentine? Love is fragile . . .

Another word is 'more'. Not very exciting this time—but let's not prejudge it. Okay, 'more' what? Bulbs? Or maybe more use out of each bulb? Eureka! Maybe we could figure out how to make a recyclable bulb, so that we could replace just the essential parts when the bulb burns out and reuse the rest. Even with compact fluorescents and LEDs, there is a lot of waste when a bulb goes out. Usually, this is because the part that stops working is packaged as a unit with other parts that don't wear out. At the very least, we could reuse the part that screws or plugs into the lamp—that part never seems to wear out. Perhaps older bulbs could have their filaments replaced with LEDs and compact fluorescents could be recharged rather than replaced. This idea comes partly from another free association: the new style of auto headlight is now made like this, with the reflector and lens built into the car, rather than (as it used to be) a large bulb. All you change is the tiny tube-like bulb inside.

We could go on, but you get the picture. Even in this simple example, just a few random word associations give us an entire set of new ideas.

After we have generated these ideas, we can begin to see some of the 'ruts' that confined our thinking originally. For instance, we tend to think of light bulbs as intact and fastened up or down—pretty much in their 'normal' shape and positions. The random prompts pushed us to consider the *ab*normal. And it turns out a few pushes were all we needed.

The raw materials for creativity are around us all the time. Prompts might come from offhand remarks or random words, a child's prattle, or odd facts about other places or times. Dreams and jokes also provide prompts, as both combine images or ideas in unexpected and suggestive ways. The challenge is to stay open to all of this. Even if they don't at first seem relevant, random prompts can help us break set, get out of our ruts, and think outside of the box.

CASE IN POINT

That our bed sheets stay in place while we toss and turn at night is, quite literally, a thing of dreams. Gisèle Jubinville, like many people, was frustrated by the challenge of getting her flat bed sheets fitted over a mattress and by the sheet's annoying reluctance to stay tucked under the mattress when finally in place. This creative Albertan set out to invent a fitted bed sheet that would go over the mattress easily when making the bed and would stay in place all night. After many hours at her sewing machine—she barely knew how to sew!—Jubinville's solution eventually came to her in a dream. She reinvented the fitted sheet. Now we are all familiar with her design: a sheet with corners that wrap under the edges of our mattresses and *stay put*.

After struggling to have her invention recognized with an official patent, which she finally got in 1990, Jubinville sold the design to an American manufacturer in 1993 (initially, none of the Canadian manufacturers were interested). It turns out hers was a million dollar dream! (Now all we need is for someone to dream up an ingenious way to fold these sheets in a tidy fashion.[7])

Another case in point: After studying at the University of Manitoba, John ('Jack') Hopps worked for the National Research Council. While in the employ of the NRC, Hopps explored various means of restoring normal body temperature to those suffering from hypothermia. He unexpectedly discovered that a hypothermic heart could be restarted by artificial means, which led to the first pacemaker in 1950.[8]

There are many other kinds of prompts too. Accidents, for example. You may know that penicillin was discovered by Alexander Fleming as the result of an accident. Fleming studied the properties of staphylococci, a kind of bacteria that can cause all sorts of health problems in humans. While stacked in his lab, some of Fleming's bacteria cultures were contaminated with mould. These cultures were ruined for the purposes of his research. Luckily, however, Fleming didn't dispose of the cultures before looking carefully enough to notice that the bacteria surrounding the mould had died-off. He determined that the contamination was a sort of fungus that produces an anti-bacterial agent. The rest is history. Sometimes you find what you are not looking for.[6]

Weather Report Blues

Now let's try the exotic association method in another, real-world, case. Let's say you are a program manager for a local TV station. You are in charge of the news and weather shows as well as other programming. You know the weather report, in particular, is dull and doesn't appeal to viewers. You need new ideas.

One problem is that weather forecasts are by nature unreliable, and the result can be frustrating. Most of us have a few choice words for weather reports when the weather does not turn out as predicted. As manager, you need to keep the weather forecast in your news program, but you know it is not boosting viewership. Indeed, you yourself find the weather report unappealing.

An obvious strategy is to seek more accurate weather information. But there are limits to this. It seems that the information you're airing is as good as it gets—but not good enough, yet, for the kind of appeal you'd like your show to have. You need to get creative in some other direction.

Once again, let's generate some random prompts. Remember, there are no strict rules—free associations can and should be random. To show how this method works, here is another example of how your thought process might go. This time the dictionary will be used as a source of prompts.

> *I'm going to flip through the 'P' section of my dictionary, free-associating as I go.*
>
> *So: 'Parcheesi'. Right. Well, Parcheesi is a game. So, could a weather forecast be presented as a kind of game (rather than a*

set of facts being conveyed)? Interesting. What kind of game? Maybe two weather reporters could compete with each other, each presenting a somewhat different forecast, and the station or the viewers could keep score?

This leads to another idea: maybe the forecast could be presented as a kind of comedy. Make it humourous—even play on the uncertainty. Maybe if it rains when the forecaster said it wouldn't, he or she should get drenched? Combining these ideas, perhaps the weather report could be formatted like a game show. Game shows can be funny and informative—they are certainly entertaining. Or, perhaps, some kind of 'reality TV' would be possible—would we follow the life of a meteorologist or reporter?

You see right away that there are some real possibilities here for generating more viewer interest. Any one of these could turn around ratings dramatically. And that's just from the first word.

'Paris.' Alright, what is the weather in Paris? Hmm . . . Would viewers be interested in that? Maybe the weather report should put more emphasis on what the weather is right now, here and elsewhere, rather than what it might be tomorrow or next week?

'Planetary.' Maybe your station could do more reporting on the movements of the planets (and moon, stars, comets, eclipses, etc.)—astronomical events that, unlike the weather, are more predictable and have their own beauty and appeal. This doesn't fix the weather forecasts themselves, but it would add something interesting that could attract viewers.

'Prime.' Prime. . . Minister. How about setting up the weather report as a debate (like political debates) between competing weather forecasters? This would create an engaging and unusual format and is ready-made for some humour. What else? Prime. . . time. This is just what we're after.

'Principal' suggests a kind of teaching. Perhaps it is possible to make weather reports a learning experience (why is the weather so complex? what are some of the factors now in play? what makes accurate predictions so difficult?), rather than mere predictions. After all, aren't there opportunities in the weather's very uncertainty? Couldn't we approach it with a spirit of adventure

and curiosity rather than just impatience? Sure, weather reports are unreliable, but why couldn't this—precisely this—make the whole business interesting?

'Prize' suggests games and competitions. How about betting, too? Maybe viewers should be allowed to call in or place online bets on the accuracy of the reports. The station could pay these off with on-the-air attention or some other benefit that also promotes the station. Or maybe when the report is wrong, the station has to give away free rain gear (of course, with the station's logo).

Again, many more ideas are possible. But let's take a few steps back from the idea-generating process to see how much our conception of the problem has changed. At first, the problem looked insurmountable—weather forecasting is just unreliable, and that's the way things are. Now, the possibilities appear to be wide open. All sorts of creative formats are possible, even if the weather reports remain unreliable. Some of the new ideas even make a *virtue* of the weather reports' unreliability. And now, most importantly, you know how to begin to generate some new ideas. It's not a matter of trying to force yourself to be more creative as if you were bench-pressing more weight. It's not a matter of more weight at all. The invitation is to a kind of playfulness instead: to get *lighter*. Thinking in *new* ways, seeking unexpected and even random stimuli, feels almost weightless. And why *shouldn't* creativity be fun?

Enough For Now—Almost

The method of inviting exotic associations is just a start. It gives us a feel for thinking in a new way. Before moving to other methods, here are a few quick guidelines and reminders for inviting exotic associations as a creative method.

First, keep an open mind with respect to the value of each prompt. It is important to avoid prejudging: don't decide that a random image or word won't suggest any useful associations until you actually give it a try. Maybe give yourself a certain minimum time—say, three minutes (you might even use a timer: three minutes may feel longer than you think)—to see what you can do with your prompt. That is, *whatever* random prompt you come up with, give it *at least* three minutes of good free-associating time. Dismissing some prompts in advance, or only half-trying with what you think is an unpromising prompt, may leave you stuck in the very rut you're trying to get out of. The prompts that seem least promising may even be your best ones because they can lead you farthest from your usual ways of thinking—but, of course, you have to be willing to follow.

Second, and for the same reason, welcome unfamiliar, ridiculous, or even taboo associations. They too can be thought-provoking—they may help you around problems that you simply can't solve head-on. Again, it's important to avoid prefiltering. There's plenty of time to filter your ideas later: the trick is to generate a lot of good material first and *then* filter it later.

Third, keep at it. Brainstormers tend to come up with the best ideas if they're asked to come up with the *most* ideas. If people are asked only to come up with the best idea they can, they will stop to fine-tune the first fairly decent idea they have. Don't stop too soon. The fourth idea, the fourteenth idea, or maybe even the fortieth idea, may be the true stroke of genius.

Finally, don't ever say 'I'm just not creative' in place of trying to do some creative thinking. Creativity is not a question of genes. Anyone can learn to be more creative. The methods are right here in this book.

CASE IN POINT

August Kekulé was a German chemist. There is an often-told story about the origins of his solution to the problem of the benzene molecule: it simply wouldn't fit the chain model of molecular structure that Kekulé had developed and that worked beautifully for describing other molecules. Kekulé struggled with this problem for seven years. One day he fell asleep in front of a fire and dreamed of serpents biting their own tails. When he awoke, he realized that the benzene molecule might not be a long chain shape but instead a *ring*. He was correct, and the vexing problem was solved. If he'd awakened annoyed, though, and said to himself 'Let me get this nonsense about tail-biting serpents out of my head and get back to my problem!' he may never have solved it.[9]

SUMMARY

The method introduced in this chapter is just one way to start thinking creatively. Getting started often requires moving ourselves out of the mental ruts in which we are comfortable thinking.

- *Break 'set'.* Avoid letting your habits and assumptions act as blinders. Be prepared to break habits and question assumptions.
- *Try Something New.* Be open to trying new methods—starting with the ones presented in this book—even those that seem improbable initially.
- *Loosen Up.* Thinking creatively requires a relaxed mind: a mind open to moving outside of one's comfort zone.

FOR PRACTICE

1. Try the following exercises to get started using the exotic association method. (You can do these exercises by yourself, or in small groups.)

   a) Imagine new uses for all sorts of everyday objects. They can be anything, even the most mundane things—dirty socks, ballpoint pens, cat litter, or whatever. Start with five objects and identify a minimum of 10 new uses for each. Remember: you are not filtering ideas yet, you are just generating as many as you can.

   b) Use random words as prompts to create new names for school or professional sports teams. (As Toronto Maple Leafs fans know, the names need not follow the usual rules of grammar or spelling.) Use the same method to create names for new restaurants.

2. Evaluate the ideas generated in exercises 1a and 1b. Are any of the ideas marketable or otherwise attractive? If they are, what makes them so? If not, use the method of inviting exotic associations to expand the list of ideas.

3. The exotic association method can be practiced on any number of everyday 'problems'. Use this method to tackle the following small but troublesome problems. Do not prefilter your lists. Include even the wildest ideas. You never know what might work.

a) Think of new ideas to deal with boredom. (It could be a boredom hotline you call to hear wild jokes, a new game, or something completely different.)

b) Generate a list of ways to travel without spending large amounts of money. Can you imagine some totally different ways to travel, or different ways to use familiar means of travel? Could youth hostels like the ones in Europe work in North America, or are there better options?

c) Create a list of new ways to deal with problems associated with i) household waste and ii) excessive power consumption.

d) Good child care is hard to find and even harder to afford for many families with young children. Apply the method of exotic association to generate possible solutions to these problems.

e) Use the method of exotic association to generate a list of at least 10 ideas to help deal with the problem of rush-hour traffic jams. (Remember to rethink the problem itself: solutions need not necessarily involve cars or roads.)

4. We often trick ourselves into thinking that the way things have been done in the past or are being done now is the way they *must* be done or the way they *ought* to be done. That is, we trick ourselves into confusing what *is* with what *is possible*. While there may be good reasons for sticking with traditions, accepting things as they are without critical reflection can also be a way to become stuck in a rut or become set in our ways of thinking. Using the method of exotic association, generate novel alternatives to the following North American practices. Push yourself to come up with really wild alternatives and remember not to prejudge. There is lots of time to consider whether the alternatives are favourable *after* you have generated a list of possibilities.

a) Celebrating in December. Many North Americans, including non-Christians, celebrate Christmas by hanging red and green decorations, writing letters to Santa Claus, and exchanging gifts.

b) Escape to Nature. Those who live in towns and cities often escape to the woods whenever they can get away from work. This practice is so common, our weekends and holidays typically begin with a long drive (complete with traffic jams) to the trail, cottage, or campground.

c) Raising Children. Typically, North American children are raised by guardians—often their parent or parents—with whom they live. What other possibilities are there? (Here you might consider both actual situations and new possibilities.)

CHAPTER THREE

MULTIPLYING YOUR OPTIONS

We have looked at one creative method in detail in order to understand what thinking outside of the box really feels like. Now you see what it takes: an adventurous attitude and a willingness to unsettle things a bit in search of new ideas and angles. It also takes a *method*.

This chapter introduces more methods for thinking creatively:

> Go Public
> Compare and Contrast
> Exaggerate!
> Mix and Match.[1]

All of these are in the same exploratory spirit as the method of exotic association.

Go Public

One great way to diversify and develop your ideas is to talk to others. Other people have had experiences we haven't had and ideas we haven't yet thought of. They may see things in ways we would not imagine. By talking to others, you are likely to gain new insights. Be prepared to ask and to listen: even a chance comment from someone else may give you a perspective you didn't have before.

Try *anyone* else. Try listening to people you've never talked to before. Listen to the people who you're sure *can't* help you. (Remember, prejudging prompts is one good way to stay in a rut.) You might even ask children for their thoughts—kids almost always have completely unexpected views and for us, they present new ways of seeing.

One specific method of 'going public' is brainstorming. Though we speak loosely of brainstorming as any attempt at creative thinking, the idea has an identifiable origin: advertising executive Alex Osborn invented it as a deliberate process to facilitate creativity in groups. (Now brainstorming is so commonplace and seems such an obvious way to generate ideas that we tend to forget that it was actually invented by someone.)

Osborn conceived of brainstorming as a technique for a group to generate a large quantity of possible solutions to a specific problem. It

KEY POINTS

Alex F. Osborn, the inventor of brainstorming, accepts the definition presented by Webster's International Dictionary. As Osborn quotes, to brainstorm is to 'practice a conference technique by which a group attempts to find a solution for a specific problem by amassing all the ideas spontaneously contributed by its members.'[2] Osborn sets out four basic rules of brainstorming. They are:

1. *Defer Criticism.* There is plenty of time to identify problems with specific ideas *after* the brainstorming session is over.
2. *Welcome every idea.* Osborn says: 'The wilder the idea, the better; it is easier to tame down than to think up.'[3]
3. *Go for quantity.* The more ideas you generate, the higher the chances are that some of them will be useful.
4. *Combine ideas.* Not only are participants encouraged to suggest new ideas, you can also brainstorm about how the ideas presented by others might be amalgamated, expanded, or improved.

works by amassing spontaneous ideas from all participants in the process. One key rule of brainstorming is to *defer criticism*. Welcome all new ideas without immediately focusing on likely difficulties or problems. In this way you give new ideas, still barely hatched, enough space to develop, to link up with other ideas, and to provoke other ideas in turn. Only *after* this process do you start addressing potential problems in your new ideas.

Of course, it's tempting (and safer) to react right away to any new suggestion with doubts: it couldn't possibly work, people won't like it, and so on. Brainstorming asks us to do the opposite: to consider how some new idea *could* work, not why it probably won't. Even what first appears to be a crude and obviously impractical idea may evolve into something much more realistic when passed around the room. It might also spark other new ideas. Ideas piggyback on each other—but you have to help that happen.

Here is an example conversation about a common problem: litter around fast-food restaurants. The exchange contains an example of simple brainstorming.

A: Maybe we'd be more likely to recycle if we realized that it takes far more energy to produce those wrappers and cans than we get out of the food or drink.

B: It does? Too bad we can't eat the wrappers and cans.

C: That's stupid.

D: Well, what if we *could* eat them?

B: Like an ice cream cone—it holds the ice cream while you eat, and then you eat the cone too. No mess.

A: Even if it got dirty, at least the dog might want it . . .

D: Dirt, huh? Maybe wrappers and cans could be made of some material that composts easily—you know, decomposes in a few weeks with water and sun.

B: You can shred up your newspapers now and put them right into the garden for mulch. Couldn't we have cans or wrappers like that?

At least two novel ideas come out of this little exchange: the idea of edible wrappers and cans and the idea of wrappers and cans that readily decompose. Both edible and decomposable wrappers are wild, but it turns out they're *realistic* ideas. Both are currently being manufactured and new developments continue.

Notice too that the process took time. It's not our job here to immediately criticize and judge other ideas, but to *work off* them to make a further association and take another step. The crucial step is to listen and to *spark*. As Osborn puts it, effective brainstorming involves *hitchhiking* on others' ideas. We started out thinking about how to get people to recycle a little more; we ended up thinking about, well, eating trash!

Poor C, though. He seems to think that his job is to pass judgment on others' ideas rather than develop or deepen them, add to them, or even offer an alternative. Reactions like C's could derail such a conversation or discourage other participants from voicing new ideas. But notice the spirit in which the others take C's comment. They keep right on thinking in a more open-ended way. The ideas keep flowing. And in the long run, C may come around too.

KEY POINTS

Imagine a meeting in which any new suggestion is met with comments like these:

- It will never work.
- We've never done it that way.
- The boss won't like it.
- If that's such a great idea, why hasn't it been done before?

In short order, no one will make any more suggestions or try to explore the ones that have been made. Defensiveness will become the name of the game, and very few ideas will be given a chance. Creative thinkers don't criticize. They ask questions instead—open-ended, exploratory, and supportive questions. Some constructive lead-ins are:

- I wonder if/why/whether . . .
- Maybe we could . . .
- That would work if . . .
- In what ways might we . . .

Edward de Bono abbreviates the last lead-in as 'IWW' ('In What Ways. . .').[4] It's a handy little acronym to put before assertions in your mind's eye (or on paper). Rather than 'People would never do this!' say instead 'In what ways might people start to do this?' Verbally it may seem like a small thing, but conceptually it is a great leap. The first statement is a categorical rejection. The second is an invitation to a joint exploration of possibilities.

Compare and Contrast

The great variety in the way people around the world live their lives offers an excellent source for new ideas. Sometimes, what seems like a strange state of affairs to us may once have been normal for a group of people somewhere and at some time in the past or even the present. We might ask this question: when we compare the way this group approaches a certain situation with the way we approach it, what can we learn from the similarities? The differences? Comparing and contrasting the way things are for us, here and now, with the way things are, or were, for other people is another method of generating new ides. This method involves learning from others without relying on the methods we discussed earlier: conversations and brainstorming. We have historical and cross-cultural comparison to learn from as well.

Did you know that Australian students can go to university first and pay later, when they have more money? Did you know that marijuana is legal in Amsterdam (and the result is not disaster)? Did you know that English toilets don't leak—whereas the flap system used in North American toilets wastes billions of gallons of water through leaks?

Other comparisons and contrasts are also available. Taxicabs and trucks in Singapore have little alarms and flashing lights that go on if the vehicle speeds. Everyone knows when you're speeding (and the cops don't need radar). Some of them are even made so they don't go off until the driver goes down to the police station and pays a fine. Why not in Canada?

Many Mediterranean countries still practice *siesta*, a period of rest and quiet in the middle of the day. Again, why not in Canada? The siesta lessens the crush of work, instead of pushing it all into a single eight-hour stretch. It might even help reduce energy consumption since the point of the siesta is to leave work during the hottest part of the day. Perhaps in Canada we could avoid the coldest part of the day in the winter months—that would be a welcome change.

Many societies had, and have, matchmakers to help young people find the right mates. This is an alternative to leaving the decision up to love or whatever other forces might pull us toward a mate. Since almost half of so-called love marriages in North America end in divorce, we might wonder if there are better ways. Canadian-born Reva Seth, for one, has argued that there are many advantages of arranged (but not forced) marriages of the sort common in other cultures.[5] There are probably some great business opportunities here—online dating services are already a multi-million dollar-a-year reality.

You see, anyway, how ideas begin to flow. We may even discover that the problems we identify are not problems at all for other people or at other times. Abortion, for example, one of the most divisive social conflicts in North America over the past thirty years, is barely an issue in most other countries (for somewhat different and sometimes opposite reasons). Even in North America, we see this remains more of an issue in the United States than in Canada.

Comparing and contrasting the way we do things with the ways others do things does not automatically generate solutions, of course, but it does give us a sense of possibility. Most problems are more open-ended than they look. We're only stuck (or only seem to be stuck) *right now*.

In order to learn from others' histories and cultures, you may need to do some research. Using the Internet as a tool, it is easy to compare historical and cultural situations to explore the differences among them. If legal marijuana is not a problem in Amsterdam, for example, why not? If brothels are tolerated in some places, like Nevada, why not in others? We shouldn't automatically assume that the only difference is a few laws. We have to consider a people's mindset, and what has brought about these cultural mores.

Exaggerate!

Exotic association is one way to create wild provocations for yourself. There are others. Remember, the aim is not to produce a usable idea immediately but to open your mind to novel possibilities, to push yourself to look at familiar things in totally unexpected ways.

Another excellent method for multiplying your options is *exaggeration*. To exaggerate, take some feature of the problem and overemphasize it. Push it as far as it can go.

To try this, take a familiar problem like people driving over the speed limit. We have seen how people in Singapore address this problem. Let's now apply the method of exaggeration to discover other possibilities. In North America, our usual response is to call for more enforcement, more cops. Creative thinking could start by exaggerating *that*: cops everywhere. Then almost everyone would have to be a cop. Perhaps there are ways in which we could all *act like* cops. What if anyone could turn in a speeder? That would require, at the least, some sort of radar in every car.

Bumps along the way might force a speeder to slow down. Suppose we exaggerate this feature of roads—what if rides get *really* bumpy at higher speeds? Crazy, right? Or maybe not. If roads were engineered so that unpleasant vibrations are set up in car frames when the speed limit is exceeded (say with a special kind of small speed bump) then roads could enforce their own speed limits. Already, textures are being added to the edges of highways to warn drivers in danger of driving off the road. What else is possible?

Wouldn't it be nice if cars themselves reminded us of some of the dangers of speed? How can we exaggerate this idea? How about re-cordings of car crashes coming over your car stereo if you hit the ac-celerator too hard? Big spikes in the middle of the steering wheel? OK, maybe not—but once again these wild and maybe even offensive ideas start us thinking. Surely there are more graphic ways to remind people, right in the car, just how dangerous speeding can be.

In the 1990s, the Canadian Government began a campaign to help reduce smoking. Now, Canadian laws dictate that cigarette packag-ing must display graphic reminders of the potential effects of smok-ing: blackened lungs, and so on. Though only one move in a complex campaign to warn people off cigarettes, declining numbers of cigarette purchases indicate this sort of campaign works. Why not, then, post similar warnings in your car?

Another use of exaggeration is what de Bono coined the method of the 'intermediate impossible'. Imagine a *perfect* solution to your prob-lem, however unrealistic. Then, work your way back to a realistic idea from there. Make your very first imaginative step a gigantic one. It's easier to tone it down later than to ramp up a timid little half-step idea into something bigger.

We have all had the frustration of misplacing our car keys. If we tackled the problem in an incremental and 'realistic' way, we might tie our keys to our clothes or purse, or look for new ways to hide spare keys outside of the car. All fine ideas. A *perfect* solution, however, would be a lot more dramatic. What if we did not need keys at all? Or what if we had the equivalent of keys that we *couldn't* misplace—say, if they were part of our bodies? We are seeing something like this al-ready. Some electric and electric-petrol hybrid cars have keys, but do not require us to insert them into the ignition. They turn on at the push of a button as long as the key is somewhere close to the button—like in the driver's pocket.

Notice that here, already, we have pushed ourselves entirely beyond questions like how to make our keys a little harder to lose. Instead, we are thinking about new kinds of keys or different practices that don't re-quire keys at all. Combination locks? Voice-recognition systems, finger-prints, even some kind of bodily imprinting? All of these are now reality.

CASE IN POINT

Albert Einstein started his professional life as a clerk in the Swiss Patent Office, capping off an undistinguished school career. He did physics in his spare time and without equipment. What he did have was imagination. And his key insights were the result of radical exaggeration. In particular, Einstein arrived at his General Theory of Relativity by imagining what it would be like to travel at the speed of light—or, to be specific, trying to figure out how the passage of time would be affected if one frame of reference were moving at or close to the speed of light relative to another. This is not exactly realistic. The speed of light is immensely greater than the speed anyone has ever traveled or perhaps ever will travel. Einstein's was a pure 'thought-experiment', but it allowed him to begin to see what we can't see when we are dealing with things from our usual perspectives in the normal world: that time passes differently depending on relative speed. Experimental corroborations came only later (and it is so hard actually to observe the relevant phenomena that there are still just a few). While we think of scientific reasoning as rational and objective, we sometimes overlook the fact that creative thinking is involved in generating most new hypotheses and theories. Equipped only with an active imagination—some of his teachers would no doubt have said *overactive*—Einstein began a revolution in physics that transformed our world.[6]

Mix and Match

Many of today's familiar products came about when separate things were combined. Pencils didn't originally have erasers. Someone imagined putting them together—when Hymen Lipman applied for a patent in the 1850s, his idea was to put the eraser *in* the end of the pencil so that both ends, the lead and the eraser, could be sharpened—and now the eraser has become so much a part of the pencil that we don't even mention it anymore. Clock radios, toaster ovens, chocolate-chip cookies, umbrella strollers—all are inventions-by-combination. Combining ideas, or mixing and matching, is another easy method for generating new ideas and identifying otherwise-overlooked possibilities.

Aspiring inventors can use the same method. Pick any two things at random and put them together. Mix and match. Let's try this right now by considering objects that might be sitting on your desk.

Postcards and a USB drive? OK, *what about a postcard that you could mail to friends to put in their computers for pictures or a video and some words from you? (Electronic or E-Cards are now common.)*

A wristwatch and a little flowerpot? *What about wearable fresh-flower holders—a new kind of jewelry? Or flowers genetically engineered to change colour on the hour?*

A stapler and a houseplant? *I don't know . . . sometimes it doesn't work! (What do you think?)*

A telephone and a calendar? *What about a single device that functions as both your phone and your day-planner? Could we add a calculator? Could we add an address book? How about a text messager or a web-browser? Really, all of this and more is built into my BlackBerry. What else could I mix with that?*

For more targeted problem-solving, take your problem, or some part of it, and do something similar: 'mix' in some quite dissimilar objects or images and see whether a useful hybrid might suggest itself.

Your problem is finding buried landmines in former war zones? Mix in, say, flowers. It turns out that researchers are already at work on certain varieties of flowers that grow fast and change colour when planted near the distinctive chemical signatures of landmines.

Your problem is how to power wells in villages without electricity? Trevor Field, a retired advertising executive and resident of South Africa, noticed that many women and children in rural settings spent hours each day fetching (often contaminated) water for their daily consumption. These circumstances left little time for the children to have fun. Mixing and matching, Field came up with the solution of creating a children's 'merry-go-round' that doubled as a water pump. Now, the kids pump water while playing! Field didn't stop there. He later added billboard advertising to the mix. Now, many of Field's 'Play Pumps' are providing a place to play, producing clean water, and generating profit by selling advertising space on the pumps' water towers.[7]

Another way to mix and match involves looking for *analogies*. This is more challenging but sometimes more powerful. Analogies can be used as the basis for building arguments, what critical thinkers call 'arguments from analogy'. They can also be used to identify possible

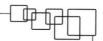

CASE IN POINT

Our 'dependence' on petroleum products has brought with it many well known problems, which include threats ranging from economic meltdowns to environmental disasters. We are all too familiar with stories of tankers running aground and spilling tonnes of oil into our oceans with catastrophic results. So, we ask, how do we clean up thousands of tonnes of oil from an ocean? An oil spill on the ocean is like any other spill only on a larger scale. How do we clean up any other spill? Most obviously, we use a towel.

An oil spill on the ocean is like the oil we get on our pans when cooking. Since oil doesn't mix with water, it floats on the ocean's surface in the same way it floats in our dishwater when we submerge a frying pan. What's more, if you play with the oil floating in your dishwater, you'll notice that oil attracts oil—the bubbles stick together. Perhaps then, we could use more oil to clean up spills in the ocean. If these ideas seem ridiculous to you, you are still thinking 'inside the box'.

A Canadian, Richard Sewell, combined these very ideas to produce what he called 'Slicklickers'. Each Slicklicker consists of a towel shaped to run like a conveyer belt. The towel is given a light coating of oil as it spins. This allows it to pick up oil from the ocean's surface without absorbing water. As the oil-soaked towel spins, it is squeezed to wring out the oil in much the same manner one would wring out a wet rag. This process is inexpensive, fast, and has the added advantage of collecting most of the oil without contamination from the ocean (an odd idea). The oil can still be used![8]

solutions to our problems. In either case, creative thinking can be used to identify analogies.

Using analogies to identify solutions to problems requires identifying new possibilities by asking whether a problem could be seen as somehow similar, or analogous, to what first appears quite different. To do this, take any problem and ask, 'How is it *like* X?' where X is some other situation or idea or object. As with the other methods introduced, this will seem awkward and strange at first, and often nothing will come of it. But startling new ways of thinking can also emerge. Think, for instance, that people had been using presses to get the juices out of grapes for centuries before Gutenberg applied the same process to printing—but no one else had made the connection.

Take the recycling issue again. By way of illustration, we can pick a few words from the day's newspaper with reckless abandon and,

CASE IN POINT

Test tubes spun in a centrifuge often break as the contents of the tubes are pushed outward. Researchers discovered that they could avoid this result by placing the test tubes inside bigger and stronger tubes filled with water. As the centrifugal force pushed the contents of the test tube outward, the extra pressure on the test tube was counteracted by the increased pressure of the water surrounding it. Creative thinking led Wilbur R. Franks, a researcher in Toronto, to experiment with applying the same solution to what might first strike us as a very different problem: airplane pilots passing out as they execute steep turns at high speeds.

As Franks recognized, the two problems are actually quite similar. The centrifugal force causing the test tubes to shatter works in the same way the gravitational (or G) forces accelerate pilots' blood toward their lower extremities and away from their brains. Franks developed a suit that surrounded pilots with water-filled bladders that counteract the pressure of the blood in the legs in the same way water counteracts the pressure of the contents of a test tube in a centrifuge. The first successful *G-suit,* as it is now known, was tested in 1941 and versions of Frank's design are still worn by aviators today.[9]

Another case in point: Canada is known for its snow. Perhaps, then, it is no surprise that a Canadian is credited with the invention of the snowblower. What is surprising, however, is that the idea for the snowblower came from another invention used exclusively in the heat of the summer.

Faced with the problem of keeping roads cleared for winter travel, Arthur Sicard was reminded of the threshers (or thrashers) he had seen used to move large amounts of grain in the summer. A threshing machine uses large rotating blades to draw grain stalks toward a central chute through which the grain travels. Moving snow, Sicard noticed, is analogous to move grain stalks. He conceived of a machine that uses blades to draw snow toward a central chute through which it is thrown out and away from roads or driveways. This concept was presented to the world in the 1920s as the world's first snowblower.[10]

without prefiltering, try to identify a few random analogies. Here's how the thought process might go:

> Religion? *How could recycling somehow be like a religious act? Maybe churches, mosques, synagogues, and temples should start serving as recycling centres. Or maybe recyclable containers should be made so precious (that is, 'sacred' in a sense) that no one would want to throw them away in the first place?*

Opera? *Could the recycling issue somehow be like opera? Well, operas are musical, obviously. So maybe we need some good recycling music. Perhaps even a whole new musical style could be associated with recycling? Could this help promote recycling?*

Making tea? *I wonder if recycling could somehow be like responding to a kettle's whistle? So... could a recyclable item somehow 'whistle' when it needs to be recycled or is being put into the wrong bin? Silly? Well, maybe it shouldn't make noise, but it could make some sort of 'statement'. How about visually? Now there's an idea: maybe we could colour-code recyclable items— say some strong shades of green—so you can tell at a glance that they are recyclable (in fact, even before you buy them) and whether you are putting them in the right or wrong bin. This seems far better than the current system of hard-to-read and harder-to-interpret numeric codes.*

Notice that we used several of the methods from this chapter and chapter 2 to arrive at this last idea. We started with an analogy, then used 'intermediate impossible' (could a recyclable item somehow whistle when it needed to be recycled?), then free-associated from there. It took a little time, but the result seems promising.

SUMMARY

The methods introduced in this chapter allow you to identify possibilities in what initially seem to be problems.
- *Go Public.* Ask around, brainstorm.
- *Compare and Contrast.* Explore how the same problem is treated in other places and at other times.
- *Exaggerate.* Go to extremes; work backward from 'perfect' solutions.
- *Mix and Match.* Try unexpected combinations and analogies.

FOR PRACTICE

1. It takes training to become comfortable using the methods for creative thinking introduced in this chapter. The following exercises are intended to help you practice these methods:

   a) Use each of the methods (Go Public, Compare and Contrast, Exaggerate, and Mix and Match) to come up with a new murder mystery plot. (How do you think the great mystery writers do it?)

   b) Use the method of Mixing and Matching and the method of Exaggeration to generate ideas for a better mousetrap. (Using random prompts to identify analogies might be especially useful here.)

   c) Identify one of the world's pressing problems. (Some examples are greenhouse gas emissions, economic crises, and natural disasters.) Use each of the four methods presented in this chapter (Going Public, Compare and Contrast, Exaggeration, and Mix and Match) to generate possible solutions to this problem.

2. *After* you have a list of 10 solutions to the problem you identify in exercise 1c, decide which of them, if any, are plausible solutions to the problem you identified. How could these solutions be implemented in practice?

3. Consider the small but troublesome daily challenges of (a) boredom, (b) inexpensive travel, (c) household waste and excessive power consumption, (d) child care, and (e) 'rush-hour' traffic jams. Apply the methods introduced in this chapter (Going Public, Compare and Contrast, Exaggeration, and Mix and Match) to generate a few possible solutions to each of these problems. Compare the lists generated using these methods to the ones you generated using exotic associations when you completed exercise 3 in Chapter 2.

4. Here are two additional problems to be addressed creatively using the methods introduced in this chapter:

   a) Staging a demonstration is one way of protesting a government's policy or practice. Yet, all too often public demonstrations do little to bring about changes in governmental policy or practice. What's more, those of us not involved in the demonstrations tend to take little notice or, if we do notice, we tend to think of them as nuisances rather than sources of information or inspiration. Using the methods introduced in this chapter, work to generate a list of alternative ways to protest governmental policy.

b) The Internet makes it possible to access all sorts of information. This includes information to which we would rather not be exposed and material that is inappropriate for children. It isn't easy to predict what children will find when they use the Internet and we are all too familiar with the limits of the various 'filters' available. Using the methods introduced in this chapter, can you identify creative means of controlling what children view when working online?

5. In our attempts to explain certain observable facts, it is tempting to accept the first plausible explanation. Using the methods introduced in this book, generate *at least four* possible explanations for each of the following sets of facts. After you have done this, consider which, if any, of the possible explanations is most plausible. Are any of your explanations so plausible you think they must be right? (If so, you have generated what critical thinkers call an 'inference to the best explanation'.)

a) Facts to be explained: My neighbours' lights are off. My neighbours own a car, but do not have a garage. My neighbours' car is not parked outside of their house.

b) Facts to be explained: Julien said he was unable to join Sarah at the movies on Saturday because he would be at home studying. Sarah saw Julien at the mall while on the way to the movies on Saturday. Julien isn't prone to lying.

c) Facts to be explained: Pictures taken by spacecraft landed on Mars and transmitted to Earth show that the surface of Mars has features that resemble dried river-beds and lakes. The pictures also show what appears to be ice in some areas. Pictures of the Martian sunsets include beautiful, wispy, clouds. (Note: more recent analysis of Martian soil has confirmed the presence of water on that planet. Does this additional fact help you identify the inference to the best explanation for the facts indicated above?)

d) Facts to be explained: My pen falls to the floor when I drop it. Every time I jump up, I come back down to the ground. Apples fall from trees when their stems become separated from the branch. The flames from my fire go up and away from the burning logs.

CHAPTER FOUR
BUILDING ON YOUR BREAKTHROUGHS

Let's suppose that you have used some of the tools we've looked at and you've arrived at an exciting and genuinely new idea about a problem that had everyone else (and maybe even you) thoroughly stuck. Don't stop now. Our single greatest temptation is to stop as soon as we make the first breakthrough, as if some sort of final exam has been passed and now there is nothing more to do. In fact, we have usually only taken the first step: we've only cracked the door open. The first breakthrough is not the end, it's where real creativity begins. Now walk through that door and keep going.

NEXT STEPS

Here are some ways to develop an idea once you make the initial breakthrough:

1. Develop your idea to meet practical challenges. Ask yourself where problems and objections are likely to come up. For example, say you want to decrease litter, and your idea is to make the containers used to ship food products so appealing that people won't throw them out. How will you do this? Perhaps you could make them refillable. Or, perhaps you could make the containers 'collectors items', thereby creating a lucrative resale market. Maybe make them reusable as building materials or toys. These are all perfectly good ideas, but still only beginnings; you can develop them further.

2. Make your original idea more specific. Clarify key terms; figure out ways to put your idea into effect and apply it to a specific situation. For example, if you want to promote recycling by creating some catchy recycling jingles, what would be a good way to do this? Maybe it would be fun (not to mention appropriate!) to 'recycle' bits of music we already know.

3. Ask yourself where your idea can go next. Fill in the details of your original idea. Starting from the idea of edible wrappers, for example, you can go on to consider what they should be made of, what they should taste like, and what colour would be most appetizing.

4. Take your first creative breakthrough and add other creative ideas about the same problem. Go right back to the tools in the previous chapters (e.g. Mix and Match and Exaggeration) to continue

CASE IN POINT

Even when we are aware of a problem and think we have a good solution, creativity can come into play. Long before Michael Moore's blockbuster documentaries, Bonnie Sher Klein was using film to promote change. Her Introduction to *Fogo Island* (National Film Board of Canada, 1968) proved that film could be effective in bringing about social change by allowing the people of a small and poor Newfoundland island to use film as a tool to build community and voice social issues. Her well-known *Not a Love Story: A Film about Pornography* (National film Board of Canada, 1981) proved invaluable in getting people to rethink problems surrounding the industry of pornography. In this film Klein and stripper Linda Lee Tracey provide a guided tour of the world of adult dancing, peep-shows, live sex acts, 'hard core' publications, and pornographic films. The anti-pornography film points to the harm caused by what was then already an eight billion dollar-a-year industry.

generating ideas, but now think about combing these new ideas with your current one to make something still more creative.

5. Take your first creative breakthrough and add other creative ideas about a different problem. As with some of the methods introduced earlier, this can feel random, but it can produce some wild and completely unexpected connections too. Try it almost mechanically: just take your problem and randomly select another problem—any problem at all—to see if there might be some cross-fertilization.

6. Extend your creative solution to other, similar problems. Barry Nalebuff and Ian Ayres call this 'solutions in search of problems'.[1] If you have a great idea about one thing, don't leave it there—ask where else it could apply. Edible wrappers, for example, might lead you to the idea of eating other things we currently throw away. Ask yourself, 'What other throwaways could be made edible too?'

TOWARD BETTER MARRIAGES

Here is one ongoing problem related to marriage: according to data available from Statistics Canada (statscan.gc.ca), more than one third of new Canadian marriages fail. The amount of unhappiness involved is staggering. What can be done to help more marriages succeed?

One suggestion for addressing the problem of failed marriages is for people to get to know each other better before getting married. This should help people identify weakness or incompatibility with potential spouses before actually tying the knot. Indeed, research by Roderick Phillips at Carleton University suggests this is one solution more and more young people are trying. The trend is toward people spending more time together and living together before marriage.[2]

This is a plausible idea—already a large step beyond the culture that tells us we can't do anything to fix the divorce rate.[3] It is the kernel of a creative solution, but in truth, it is also just a starting point. The idea that people should get to know each other better before they are married could be far more powerful if we build on it in some of the ways just outlined. Let us first try to make the initial idea more specific. How could it be put into practice?

An initial suggestion might be to change the marriage laws to add the requirement that couples cannot marry until they have known each other for, say, at least a year. This should cut down on hasty marriages and eliminate the pressure some young people feel to marry right away if a relationship feels right. The cultural message would be to slow down, take your time, make sure this is the right person.

Good so far. But questions arise again—and considering them systematically is, as we discussed in chapter 2, another way to go farther . One question is 'How could such a rule be enforced?' Another is 'How could you prove you'd known each other long enough?' Besides, many couples in marriage-like relationships (what Canadians call 'common law' or Australians call 'de facto' marriages) don't in fact take part in any legally recognized marriage ceremony, but breaking up is still legally and emotionally difficult. Maybe we need something more than, or different from, changing marriage laws.

If we agree that people really should get to know their prospective spouses better before getting hitched, how could we promote or enforce this? To move forward, let's try a few random prompts.

All right, let's try 'community'. Do couples and families sometimes get too self-involved to think enough about community service? Perhaps we could add incentives for people to help more outside the family unit. To be specific: could an idea about 'more service' somehow go together with the idea about 'getting to know you before marriage'?

At first glance, no: they are two separate ideas. But wait a minute. What about community service as a way of getting to know a potential spouse? The idea would be to do the service work together. After all, getting to know someone is not just a matter of time. You could spend a year having delightful dates and vacations but have no clue whatsoever what your potential spouse is like under pressure, at work, or with children. To really get to know someone, you need to see and interact with that person in less than ideal settings and under stress.

There you have it, then. People could be encouraged to do community service work together as a way of doing some good in the community and also of getting to know a potential spouse better. Being totally absorbed in each other is nice when you're in love, but it doesn't help much in getting ready to have children or building compatible careers. Service work is a way to be absorbed together in something bigger. Think of the enormous benefit to community service organizations— soup kitchens, environmental clean-ups, you name it—if large numbers of good-hearted people made a regular practice of helping out. Think of the long-term benefits if people associated this kind of work with *romance*! And think of all the bad marriages prevented and good marriages cemented in this way.

Notice, too, that this proposal also addresses another problem related to the original suggestion. This was the problem of proving you and your partner have in fact known each other for the requisite year (or whatever period your new rules might require). This would be easy if there were records for community service.

In the end, though, we may decide that community service is not the best way to address the problem of failed marriages—it might not even be part of a good solution. What should be clear is that we are in a better position to evaluate our idea against other possibilities now that we've done some work with it.

Going back to the initial idea that people should really get to know their prospective spouses better before getting married, we might now explore another way of moving forward. Let's build on this idea in a different direction by further exploring Reva Seth's suggestion (mentioned in Chapter 3) that certain advantages of arranged marriages could be realized in North America.

CASE IN POINT

The transit system in Whitehorse is an especially interesting result of creative thinking. A group known in Yukon as the 'Women's Mini-Bus Society' formed in 1975 to address a specific problem: a lack of public transit in Whitehorse.

For the most part, the Society included those most affected by the lack of public transit in Yukon's capital city—married women committed to caring for children at home without access to a car. Some of these women didn't own cars at all. Others didn't have access to a car because their husbands used the family car to get back and forth to work each day. Especially during the cold Yukon winters, these women found themselves without easy means of getting around town. Their creative solution was to start a transit system that served their specific transportation needs.

Led by Joyce Hayden, the Women's Mini-Bus Society built on its initial idea by looking for creative solutions to a number of practical challenges. In the end, the Society successfully procured government grants, purchased mini-buses, and performed all of the services to keep the buses going—including maintenance tasks and driving. In so doing, the society created another service: jobs with hours tailor-made for women with other (often family-related) responsibilities. In less than five years, the value of the transit service was clear and an independent transit commission was formed to further develop the system.[4]

In some cultures a matchmaker pairs up two young people to be married. For instance, in some Asian and Middle Eastern countries, the matchmaker—this can be a person or small group of people—weighs advantages and disadvantages of pairings before arranging a suitable marriage. Employing such matchmakers would be a radical change from the norm in North America. But, we might ask, where's the romance in this?

Adopting practices that realize the advantages of arranged marriages need not exclude romance. Maybe people who are already attracted to one another could engage in a process to determine whether they are also likely to survive as a married couple. Maybe something like the pre-marriage classes offered by some churches could be made mandatory for all affianced couples.

And there are other questions to which answers are needed. We need to decide, for instance, who is to play the role of the matchmaker. Here again, there are many possibilities. If a third party acts as the match-maker, who might this third party be? Perhaps the matchmaker could be another person, or it might be a computer program of the sort used by eHarmony.ca and other online dating services.

Already we have made our initial idea more specific. We started with the idea that people should get to know each other better before getting married. And the way in which we are now building on this idea is certainly different than the community service idea.

Another option is for people to serve as their own matchmakers. Sound crazy? Allowing the individuals in question to act as match-makers is one way to realize the advantages of an arranged marriage—especially the consideration of advantages and disadvantages of the pairing—without taking the freedom to select a mate away from the individuals. Free choice is certainly something we value in North America.

But isn't this what we have already? Aren't people already choosing their own partners? In a way, yes, though obviously our current methods for selecting a mate are far from perfect. We can go farther. What specific selection process should we employ? Perhaps we could allow people to serve as their own matchmakers while requiring that they interview one another in the presence of another person before the marriage license is granted. During the interviews, people who are attracted to one another could be required to ask each other about their values, past experiences, habits, goals, ambitions, and other important factors affecting the success of marriages.

Far from absurd, this idea is moving us from the radical suggestion that we should endorse marriages arranged by someone other than the people to be married toward something closer to what already takes place (or should already take place) in North America. We hope that couples will discuss these things before they commit to one another, but the high rate of divorce suggests many people don't think enough about whether their mate is a good match. Forcing couples to discuss these matters would certainly be new.

There are other practical problems that would need to be addressed too. For one thing, we would have to find ways to enforce the completion of these interviews. For another, we would have to decide what to do if people wish to be married without engaging in the match-making process.

What other problems can we anticipate? In asking this question, we have made a good start. There is a great deal of room to continue moving forward.

WHAT'S IN A NAME?

A smaller, but persistent, problem related to marriage concerns the selection of a married name. North Americans—especially North American women—are influenced by many factors when deciding on a married name. Not the least of these is that adopting a husband's surname is traditional: it is what's expected, it is what some people consider proper, and, in many ways, it is more convenient than other options. Yet, there are serious reasons for moving away from the tradition too. For one thing, many of us are attached to our names as part of our identities. Since a person's sense of self is often tied to her name, pressure to abandon her original name might be perceived as a loss of part of her identity. For another, our names are often important because we are known by them in our professions. What's more, this tradition has unequal results: men aren't required to give up anything.

In recent decades, many married women have chosen to keep their original surnames. But this has other problems. Aside from challenging traditional societal expectations, it might be considered a slight to the couple's new, shared identity. And in many ways, it is more convenient when a couple shares one name socially. Are there better options? Among other things, an ideal alternative would have to be equitable and would need to reflect each person's identity both as an individual and a member of a new family.

There are, of course, options beyond either adopting a husband's surname or keeping one's original surname. Some men reverse tradition by taking their wife's surname. Some couples work to generate new, shared names. Hyphenating names is another egalitarian alternative, but it often produces unwieldy results and can be burdensome when carried to the next generation. Another possibility is that each person could adopt the other's surname as a middle name. Surely, other solutions are available: can we think of something better?

Opening our minds to other possibilities is as easy as using the methods introduced in Chapters 2 and 3 again. We could generate exotic associations from random prompts, for instance, or compare and contrast. Comparing the dominant tradition in North America with the traditions of people in earlier times and in other places sheds light on many different possibilities. The dominant practice in Canada and the United States resembles practices that became common in France and England about 1000 years ago. Global and historical comparisons reveal a variety of other practices.

Whereas we tend to use a family name as a surname, the Icelandic tradition dictates that each child's last name be derived from the first name of the father (usually) or mother. Following this practice, any son or daughter of Erik would have the last name Eriksson or Eriksdóttir where '-son' indicates the child is Erik's son, and '-dóttir' indicates the child is Erik's daughter. (The phone directory in Iceland is organized alphabetically by given name.) By law, most Icelandic people retain their original last names when married.[5]

Whereas we tend to place our given name before our surname, the opposite is done in countries including China, Hungary, and Japan. We tend to think in terms of 'first', 'last', and 'middle' names. The tradition in Spain is for each person to have two surnames—the first of these is the father's first surname and the second is the mother's first surname. In our terms, this would amount to having two 'last' names. Following this convention, all children of Juan Garcia Rodriquez and Maria Alvarez Medina will be given the last names Garcia Alvarez. Typically, Spaniards do not abandon their birth names when they are married. The Spanish tradition, for one, allows individuals to maintain the same name whatever their marital status. What's more, children's names reflect membership in both their mother's and their father's family. Would we be better to adopt a convention like this? Are any of these alternatives better than our own traditions?

Even in Canada, we find different conventions. A woman living in Alberta can choose to change her last name to her husband's (either alone or in combination with her maiden name) and use her married name on her credit cards, her driver's license, and other legal documents. The Government of Alberta does not, however, consider this a legal change: the woman's birth certificate remains, of course, unchanged even if she decides to have the name changed on other documents. A married woman can go back to using the name on her birth certificate at any time in that province.[6] Similar conventions are found in many, but not all, other provinces.

Changes to Quebec's civil code in 1981 make clear that women must keep their original last names when they are married. In that province, people may choose to adopt a spouse's name socially, but not legally—each person must use their 'birth' name on driver's licenses, health cards, and other legal documents. Even married women who move into Quebec from other provinces are required to use their original surname on their driver's licenses and other legal documents (whether or not they had adopted a new name at the time they were married).[7]

Changes to the laws in Quebec were considered an avant garde attempt to promote equality. Despite this, some consider the strict requirement to maintain one's original surname an inconvenience. Some women would prefer to have the choice of changing their names even if some of the reasons for doing so are tied to traditional, and unequal, practices.[8]

Comparing the way people are named in different cultures (even across our own country) makes clear that our practice is one convention among many. There are other ways to do things. They can work too. Having identified different possibilities, the next step is to build on some of our ideas. This time, let's start with the idea that marrying people choose their own, new, shared name. This is but one of the many ideas we have identified—we could have chosen any of them for further exploration. Indeed, we should build on as many of the ideas as we can before deciding which is best.

The initial idea is that when two people get married they would no longer be, say, John Smith and Claire Bernier but John X and Claire X, where X is the new common name they choose. This is exactly what Lindsay Milakovic and Ian Goodhue decided to do: the couple from Toronto changed their names to Lindsay and Ian GoodTimes when married in 2009.[9] With this, the GoodTimes have realized a more egalitarian system than what is traditional. The GoodTimes also realized the chance to be creative in naming themselves. On the down side, following this practice would mean that married people no longer share any names with their parents or other birth-family members—possibly a problem, though on the traditional naming system this is already true of those married women who take their husbands' surnames. We also presume that children would take the new, created, name as their last name.

Though novel, this approach is not outrageous. Can we push it further? How can we develop this idea? For one thing, we might ask if there is some way we could have the advantages of the new system—spouses readily sharing a name in an equitable manner—with at least some of the advantages of the traditional way. Can we push this idea in a way that allows room for names to be shared across generations? Can we push this idea to realize other advantages still? Since people often do come to identify with their original names, it would be nice to have a naming system that allowed everyone a little more continuity.

We might wonder if a better solution would be for married people to hold onto their original name while adding a new married name (that is, rather than simply changing names). Actually, this would not be hard to do: their married name could become their new last name and their original last name could become their middle name, John Smith and Claire Bernier would become John Smith X and Claire Bernier X. And the kids would simply be Mario or Maxine X.

This is plausible. It accomplishes more of what we want. Everyone would still share a name with both parents, and parents with children; spouses would share a (single) name with each other. It asks no more of a name change—in fact, it asks less—than most women are pressured toward by traditional arrangements.

Couples could also take a new married name as a middle name, while retaining their original last name. John Smith and Claire Bernier would become John X Smith and Claire X Bernier. The kids could still be Mario or Maxine X.

Would this be better than our current practice? Maybe, maybe not. It would take more getting used to. We are conditioned to think of adding new names only at the end of our existing names rather than at the start or in the middle. Perhaps we could move toward something more like the Spanish tradition by treating both the new, shared, name and the original names as 'last' names—whether the created name is placed before or after each spouse's original surname. Either way, people would keep their original names and just expand them a little, and could choose to use both surnames in some settings and only one in others.

As a parent at school relating to my kids, I might use only my married name, the name I share with them. At work, mostly, my original name might be enough. This scheme still allows people to share a name with both their spouses and their children, and with both their parents, with the additional advantage that they can keep their names upon marriage.

We have now built on our original idea by thinking about some of its practical implications such as how this would affect the naming of children. As a result, we are in a better position to decide whether this idea is one we would want to adopt. Before we stop, though, we ought to ask whether we can do still better. Again, take your time, don't stop too soon. What other options are there?

In deciding how best to address the problem about married names, we might also reconsider 'the' problem itself. Though the tradition in which a woman takes her husband's name has been challenged in recent decades, the prevailing attitudes remain firm. One recent survey of citizens in the United States (there is a lack of data concerning attitudes of Canadian citizens) indicates that more than 70 per cent (at a low estimate judging by other surveys) of Americans think that a woman should adopt her husband's surname at the time of the marriage.[10] Indeed, the majority of these people thought that this should be made mandatory by law. Researchers indicate that most participants surveyed thought it was a joke when asked whether men should be made to adopt their wives' surnames.

Instead of asking whether a woman should take her husband's surname, we might ask, 'What purpose is, or purposes are, served by our surnames?' This is a different question. Answering it might lead us to better ways of approaching the first question.

It is easy to identify reasons for our current ways of using surnames. For one, the use of surnames helps us identify specific individuals without confusion. This is especially helpful in communities large enough to have more than one Sarah, Thanh, Mathieu, or Mahmoud. The use of surnames also helps to make manageable written records—be they records of birth and deaths, or even lists of the sort we find in the phone book.

Whatever the historical reasons for adopting surnames, they can serve also to denote an individual's membership in a family and, perhaps, the wider community. For most people, our names are tied to our identity as members of social groups.

Are there other possibilities here? If naming were simply an issue of 'labeling' each person, it would be easy to standardize a system in which we assign each person a unique label or code. What's more, these 'names' could be designed to include all sorts of information—our genetic relations, our date and place of birth, unique identifying features, and so on. And, assuming these codes are not fixed, they could also be designed to indicate other things like our family or community groups, our marital relationships, the number of offspring we have, and so on. Something like this was used by the Canadian government to 'name' Inuit in the 1940s. Each individual was given a disk, which was supposed to be worn, with a unique letter and number sequence identifying the specific region in which the individual lived and distinguishing the individual from others within that region. These 'disk' numbers were intended to allow accurate record keeping—something deemed too difficult using traditional Inuit names. Not only are there no traditional surnames, but given names are often passed along from generation to generation (and from male to female or female to male) without change.

It is, of course, easy to anticipate most people's receptivity to replacing their names with codes of the sort found on products, spines of library books, license plates (even if personalized), or the striped jumpsuits of inmates. Are there other possibilities that are more plausible?

Again, we might rethink 'the' problem concerning married names in a different way. Since the problem is tied to marriage, we can go further by exploring the possibility of rethinking marriage altogether—is some other arrangement possible that would carry the same values (stability, commitment, family, etc.)? This is certainly a different question than the one we started with!

We do not need to decide between only these options. More important is simply to recognize them—and in particular realize that a more subtle but perhaps somewhat preferable option could be overlooked easily if, for instance, we fasten too quickly onto the more obvious last-name option. Give it time.

Sometimes we will decide that none of our creative 'solutions' is better than the 'problem' we have. In these cases, the result of our creative process might be to endorse a conservative approach—change for the sake of change is not always a good idea. As creative and critical thinkers, this is a judgment we will make only after considering other possibilities with an open mind. That is, only after we have given creativity a chance.

In other cases, we will decide that a change in tradition or practice would be good. In these cases, our task is to build on our breakthrough until all of the practical details are addressed. How could we convince others to adopt our idea? If we did decide a new system of naming was in order, would the new system be mandatory by law? How would our idea affect existing records? Would the system be applied retroactively: would previously married couples be forced to change their names? There is room for creative answers to each of these additional questions.

SUMMARY

The methods introduced in this chapter take your initial creativity a step further: they ask you to build on the ideas generated by thinking creatively. Building on your breakthroughs often can be accomplished by using the same methods as those used to generate the initial ideas:

- *Don't Stop*. Avoid the impulse to stop with your first good idea. Often a good idea can become a better idea with further creative thinking.
- *Clarify Your Idea*. Build on a breakthrough idea by thinking about the practical details.
- *Use Your Methods. . . Again*. In developing your ideas, apply the methods of creative thinking again. This time, part of your challenge is to generate creative ways of expanding on your initial breakthrough. This is a different problem than the one you started with.
- *Be Patient*. Sometimes seeing whether or how a new idea could work takes time. Build on your breakthroughs before deciding whether each idea is good or practical.

FOR PRACTICE

1. Even the most promising ideas often demand a good deal of work before they can be implemented. This work can involve creative thinking in the form of building on our breakthroughs. The following exercises will help you to identify the need and value of building on initial ideas.

Design a new board game. You may know that two Canadian journalists, Scott Abbott and Chris Haney, conceived of the idea for Trivial Pursuit in less than one hour. The game was on the market three years later and has made quite a profit for the inventors. Put the methods introduced in Chapters 2 and 3 to use in designing a new board game. Once you have an idea for a new game, build on your breakthrough by identifying the practical challenges you would face if you wanted to sell your game. Consider how it would be marketed and to whom, how it would be manufactured, and so on.

Design a completely new business. Begin by identifying a real need that is not now being met. (If this has you stumped, put the methods from the earlier chapters of this book to the test again.) The need you identify will be your breakthrough, but it is only a beginning. To build on the breakthrough, use creative thinking to design a business that will meet this need. Consider what good or service you will offer, how you will market it, and so on.

2. This chapter presents possible solutions to existing problems surrounding the institution of marriage—specifically, problems related to married names and the high rate of failed marriages. The solutions presented are just a beginning. Apply the methods introduced in this chapter to go farther with the ideas being proposed and to generate new solutions to these problems. What are some other problems related to marriage? Can you think of ways of addressing them too?

3. One problem we face in resolving the ongoing debate about the legal status of same-sex relationships is tradition: the traditional definition of marriage is thought to specify that marriages are between one man and one woman. Are there other problems we face in resolving the debate about the legal status of these relationships? How about the naming problem—certainly the traditional model won't apply in same-sex unions. Can you imagine ways of responding to these problems?

4. The exercises in the previous chapters put before you a wide range of problems, and challenged you to make some creative breakthroughs with each one of them. Consider again some of the ideas you generated to deal with (a) boredom, (b) inexpensive travel, (c) household waste and excessive power consumption, (d)

child care, and (e) 'rush-hour' traffic jams. Choose your best idea for addressing each of these problems and take it farther using the methods introduced in this chapter. How would you implement the solution to each problem? What challenges would you face?

5. Laws dictate that people in Canada and the United States must drive on the right-hand side of the road. People drive on the left-hand side of the road in many other countries. Imagine a scenario in which the Government of Canada decided it was a good idea to have everyone drive on the other, that is the left-hand, side of the road from now on. Build on this idea using the methods introduced in this chapter. Start by identifying potential problems and work to supply creative solutions. (If you are stuck, you might do a quick search for information about the many countries that have made similar changes. Most recently, the people in Samoa started driving on the left side of the road rather than the right—in large part, this was to make their practices consistent with those of other nations in the area. In the 1960s and 1970s, similar changes occurred in Iceland, Sweden, and Ghana to name a few.)

CHAPTER FIVE

REFRAMING PROBLEMS

When faced with problems, often our instinct is to go straight to looking for solutions. Sometimes there are better ways to address problems—better ways to take them up—than 'solving' them in the straightforward ways we have so far considered. Looking for solutions is not always the most creative response. So, some major steps remain to be taken in our survey of the realm of creativity. This chapter introduces three alternative ways of approaching problems.

Think Laterally

A straight line is not always the best way between two points. What if there were a steep wall or an unfriendly dragon in the way? Rather than charging directly ahead into a problem, then, we also need to look for sidesteps and alternate routes. We need to revisit every part of a problem, not just the one or two seemingly most obvious aspects. Each aspect of a problem can be varied, questioned, and stretched. This is 'lateral thinking'. It is the sort of thing we started to do at the end of the previous chapter when we asked whether the problems related to married names could be addressed by rethinking the purposes of our names or by rethinking marriage itself.

Consider the story about a group of friends who were swimming together in a creek when suddenly one of them became tangled in some underwater vines. Struggling desperately, he couldn't get to the surface; he remained a foot under. His friends dove again and again to try to untangle him, but it quickly became clear that they could not get him free in time.

One friend thought: if he can't get to the air, maybe the air can get to him. Right on shore was a homeowner with a garden hose and pruning shears. Two snips later and she had a two-foot length of hose. She had a makeshift snorkel! The trapped swimmer was saved by a friend who shifted her attention to one aspect of the problem that was more easily solved.[1] He literally owes his life to lateral thinking.

Remember, too, the well-known story about the ancient scientist Archimedes. The king of the day had given his metalsmith some gold to make a crown. The king came to suspect, though, that the smith took some of the gold for his own enrichment and substituted silver instead. Archimedes got the job of finding out.

KEY POINTS

Thinking laterally involves rethinking problems before, and sometimes in lieu of, looking for solutions. This requires creativity and, with some practice, it is easy to do. Here are a few questions to get you started:

- What, exactly, is the problem? *Is the problem that the boy is under water or is the problem that he can't access air to breathe?*
- What would constitute a 'perfect' solution? *Remember, from Chapter 1, 'the problem' of deciding who you should give a ride in your two-seater car.*
- Why is this a problem? *Identifying the root of a problem can go a long way toward identifying a creative solution.*
- What change(s) would eliminate the problem? *Getting rid of our cars would eliminate 'rush-hour' traffic as we know it. What else could we change?*

If Archimedes knew the volume of the crown, he could take an equal volume of solid gold and weigh the two against each other: if the crown came out lighter, he'd know it was partly silver. But here was the rub: how could he measure the volume of something so lacy and finely worked? He could hardly just melt it back down, and calculation would take a lifetime. What could he do?

Archimedes went to the public baths one day, this problem weighing on his mind, and at the moment of lowering himself into one of the tubs, water splashing over the sides, he found his lateral solution. The volume of any solid object equals its displacement in water. He could measure it indirectly. All he needed to know was how much water the crown displaced. This was when, as the story goes, Archimedes ran home naked—too excited to put on his clothes—shouting '*Eureka!*' at the top of his lungs.[2]

Modern scientists face similar challenges, and lateral thinking continues to offer unexpected solutions. Astronomers suspect that planets orbit other stars, for instance, but they're extremely difficult to see in even the best telescopes. Their light is very dim, and they are massively outshone by their suns. The solution: look not for the planets themselves but for the wobble their gravity causes in their star's movement. Again, we see lateral thinking at work.

CASE IN POINT

Suppose you are an engineer for the Canadian Space Agency working on the next *Phoenix Mars Lander*. This is the craft that carries the Canadian-designed and manufactured meteorological station used to record and transmit vital weather statistics from Mars' surface to earth.[3] The problem is that the Martian surface is rocky in many places, and a lander that came down on a boulder field could easily tip over or get wedged between rocks, damaging the craft and making it impossible to deploy solar panels or antennas—and there goes $500 million down the drain. It's happened.

Though mission planners can select appropriate landing spots and design thrusters and other means of controlling the speed of descent, none of these are foolproof. Any number of variables can affect a successful landing. To add to the challenge, Mars is too far away for remote-controlled landings.

Instead of trying to solve the problem of ensuring a perfectly soft landing in a flat and unobstructed area, creative thinking can be employed to generate a lateral solution. In this case, a team of the world's top rocket scientists opted for a highly creative, but low-tech, solution. They decided to equip the lander so that it is better able to withstand a 'hard' landing at any point on the planet and then settle in an area suitable to begin the exploration mission: just the sort of thing a beach ball will do if thrown in a big yard. Beach balls don't require expensive Artificial Intelligence. With gravity and a little time, a beach ball will bounce along until it settles in a relatively level site.

NASA's approach to designing Mars Landers is analogous. When the *Mars Pathfinder* (1997) and two *Mars Exploration Rovers* (2004) landed, they were surrounded by specially designed airbags. The *Mars Exploration Rovers* looked much like oversized bundles of white grapes as they landed—not too far off from beach balls. The rovers bounced across the planet's surface in their airbag cushion until coming to rest on relatively flat terrain. After this, the 'balls' deflated and the rovers were ready to explore.[4]

NASA may even extend the beach ball concept to design the next generation of rovers. Instead of using a golf cart–like powered rover, the idea is to design something that the Martian winds could blow around, like tumbleweed or beach balls. This idea was presented to a group of sixth-graders for further inquiry in collaboration with a North Carolina State University engineering class under contract with NASA. Their challenge is to imagine ways to make the tumbleweed idea practical.[5] This goes to show that while creative thinking is certainly not rocket science, rocket science can benefit from creative thinking! And, when you're stuck, ask a sixth-grader.

Dr Theresa ('Terry') Allen, at the University of Alberta, claims that '[m]ost of the best discoveries were made by serendipity. Discoveries can't be forced; they come when you put two different ideas together.'[6] This doesn't mean that we shouldn't work with specific questions and problems in mind. And, as Professor Allen's own work reflects, sometimes the best answers come only after moving away from the usual questions.

The usual approach in fighting cancer is to look for new and effective drugs. 'Most people think "Oh, we have to discover another new drug."' Instead, Allen and her colleagues 'decided to take an existing anti-cancer drug and find a new way of delivering it'. The new, so-called *stealth* technology delivers drugs for chemotherapy to the site of the cancer using liposomes (think of soap bubbles filled with the chemotherapy drug that travel through the blood and 'pop' when they reach damaged blood vessels surrounding tumours) without being rejected as a foreign substance along the way. The result is a way to fight cancer by making existing drugs more effective while minimizing the side effects.[7] Similar developments using polymers to deliver drugs are being made by the L'Oréal-UNESCO Women in Science prize winner, Dr Eugenia Kumacheva, at the University of Toronto.

The Problem Is the Opportunity

After purchasing a drug store in Toronto, William Knapp Buckley concocted the first of his now famous cough suppressants. This was in 1919. As Buckley's company struggled to compete with larger drug companies in the 1960s and 1970s, W.K.'s son, Frank, decided to emphasize the mixture's most remarkable qualities: its effectiveness in treating coughs and its terrible taste. Both the positive and the negative were presented in what has become one of the most successful advertising campaigns in North America. Now everyone knows, 'It tastes awful. And it works.' By emphasizing what seemed to be a problem, sales of *Buckley's Mixture* sky-rocketed.[8] This is an excellent example of lateral thinking.

We label situations as 'problems' when something comes up that threatens to disrupt or complicate the plans we are following. But this label can be a trap, blinding us to the possibilities in those very situations. Maybe the 'problem' instead, like the awful taste of *Buckley's Mixture's*, is an opportunity. Heinz has done something similar in marketing its ketchup. That Heinz ketchup is difficult to pour (which was initially seen as a problem) has been spun to reflect the very image of a high-quality product—surely, we are to believe, thick Heinz ketchup is better than that runny stuff manufactured by their competitors! Instead of trying to get rid of such 'problems', in short, we should ask how we can make use of them. This is a second method for reframing problems. Let's call it opportunism.

Take Chapter 1's buried rock one more time. First we wanted to move the rock. Then we wanted to move the building—that's the lateral step. But finally we decided to *use* the rock to build a better building. The rock itself turned out to be a solution rather than a problem; an opportunity to create (redesign) a far better and truly fabulous structure using the rock itself for a dramatic feature.

Here is another example. Frontier College began in 1899 when Alfred Fitzpatrick of Nova Scotia devoted himself to addressing the problem of illiteracy. As Fitzpatrick realized, tackling the problem of illiteracy involved many other challenges. People have families, jobs, and the responsibilities that go along with families and jobs. People who can't read are no exception, and learning to read takes a considerable time commitment. What's more, Frontier College depends on the involvement of volunteer teachers and these volunteers can't be expected to give up everything to accommodate the working schedules of their students. Fitzpatrick's creative solution was to generate two possibilities at once: jobs for volunteers and education for people with jobs. During the day, teachers work alongside their students wherever these people happen to work—in a plant, on a farm, in a mine, wherever. For this, they are paid (albeit usually minimum wage). After work, the roles are altered and the teachers become volunteers, helping the students become more proficient readers. Rather than trying to get people to go to school, Frontier College brings the school to the people and creates a new opportunity in the process. Though the literacy rate has improved in Canada since the late ⹁300s, Frontier College remains active using the model resulting from Fitzpatrick's creative thinking.[9]

Many environmental issues lend themselves to opportunistic rethinking too. Take recycling, for example. In nature, what's waste for one species is resource for the next. Trees make use of the carbon dioxide we exhale, as we make use of the oxygen they exhale. So couldn't we begin to think that way about the massive waste in our own system? Why not look at trash as a kind of raw material?[10] Building materials account for approximately 40 per cent of landfill volume in North America. Why not recycle them into new construction and, from now on, make building materials to be easily recycled?

Or again, power plants create 'excess' heat, which usually is dissipated into the air or water, often at great cost. But couldn't that heat be used for something? How about home heating? There you have the origins of *cogeneration*, in which power companies also market hot water to surrounding communities—reducing the cost of both power and heat.

Try Prevention

Everyone knows that it's better to stay healthy than to wait until you get sick and then have to deal with the illness. We don't always act on this knowledge, but we do know it. Taking daily vitamins is a lot wiser

CASE IN POINT

When Henry Ford was setting up the first assembly lines to build the Model T, his suppliers received very specific requests about how to build the boxes in which they sent their bolts or cushions. A certain kind of wood had to be used, cut to certain sizes, with holes drilled just in certain places. Puzzled, but anxious for Ford's business, they complied. It turned out that once the boxes were unpacked at the assembly line, they were taken apart and used for the Model T's floorboards. They were already cut and drilled in just the right ways. Ford *could* have posed 'the' problem simply as, 'How do we get rid of excess boxes?' No one would have seen the box as anything but litter. Instead, Ford asked, 'What could the box be used for?' Instead of becoming litter, the excess box material became an opportunity. Ford was able to take two problems—procuring floorboards and getting rid of unwanted boxes—and turn them into one solution. Reuse (or 'next use') was planned into the very design of things. Some thinkers now call this 'precycling'. We could use a lot more of it.

than waiting until you get a cold and then pulling out the deconges-
tants and throat lozenges (and suffering anyway). Folk wisdom knows
it too: 'An ounce of prevention is worth a pound of cure'. This was one
reason behind the Government of Canada's campaign to reduce the
consumption of cigarettes.

This same way of thinking can be a form of creativity as well. The
strategy is the same. Think preventively, 'proactively'. Don't just take
the problem for granted—ask whether it even needs to come up in the
first place. Look to its causes. What is the problem behind the problem,
so to speak? Is there a way to rearrange things so that we don't get
stuck with this problem, or anything like it, at all? How, at least, can
we keep it from coming up so often and/or in so difficult a form?

Consider this snippet from *The New York Times:*

> Recently a mother complained to me that her 9-year-old daughter
> watches television for eight hours a day and she couldn't get her
> to stop. 'Why not?' I asked. 'Because,' the woman answered, 'the
> TV is in her bedroom.'[11]

You can imagine the usual parent–child fights. You can even imagine other creative solutions, like rewards for keeping the TV off or
agreed weekly viewing schedules. But best of all, obviously, would just
be to take the TV out of the child's room. What's striking is that this
solution apparently never even crossed the mother's mind. Sometimes
we need help.

With new technologies often come new moral problems. Recent ad-
vances in medical technology allow us to keep people's bodies alive
even when their brains have stopped working. In some cases, families
pleaded to let these people die but, since the law wasn't clear whether
the plug could legally be pulled, the bodies were kept going, sometimes
for years, at incredible economic and emotional cost.

Usually in this kind of situation there is no easy answer—there are
no happy outcomes. And, there is significant disagreement about which
answer is morally best. It isn't clear what serves the interests of people
on life-support and they cannot express any preference to die or to be
kept going. Since the early 1990s, courts in Canada have recognized
the validity of advanced directives or living wills. It is now common
that people declare their desires before the subject arises, often to say

that they do not want to be kept alive in a brain-dead condition. Lawyers are satisfied and the controversy has been lessened immensely. Again, 'an ounce of prevention. . .'.

Fertility clinics are doing something similar to avoid problems. When these clinics started storing couples' fertilized embryos, they found themselves in huge battles if couples split up. Which partner 'owned' the embryos? We were headed for decades of contentious cases wending their ways through the courts. The clinics, wisely, took a very different and preventive approach. Now, before they accept an embryo at all, they ask each couple to designate one or the other as the embryo's 'owner' in the event of divorce. No more problem! (This is not even an ounce of prevention—more like a milligram—but it does the trick.)

Or take the problem of speeding once again. We've considered some unusual responses, such as putting flashing lights on top of speeding cars or spikes on the steering column. One thing we have not done, though, is to ask why people speed in the first place. Couldn't we also cut down on speeding by addressing or removing its causes? What would prevention look like here?

One precondition for speeding is that cars are able to go much faster than speed limits. One ridiculously simple idea to cut down on speeding, then, would be to stop making cars that can go so fast or to build in some sort of speed-control system. In Canada, Quebec and Ontario have passed laws requiring every tractor-trailer to have a speed limiter (or 'governor') set so that the truck can travel no faster than 105 km/h. This should make the roads safer. It will also have environmental advantages by reducing fuel consumption and the related pollutants. Similar laws are now in place in the EU and Australia.

One reason to speed is because we find ourselves running late for work. Once again, this readily suggests a few unexpected but totally logical means of prevention. Leaving for work a little earlier, for one. Likewise, we'd be less rushed if we simply scheduled our first meetings and classes a little later.

And why not apply this more generally? For many jobs, we could institute a system of 'flex-time' where work begins when you show up, rather than requiring you to show up at a set time. At one stroke this reduces the time pressures created by a rigid work schedule. People would no longer have to speed to arrive on time.

Notice once again that this is a different kind of problem-solving. We are no longer taking the problem as fixed and simply trying—however creatively—to cope. Now we are reframing 'the' problem itself. Not surprisingly, then, other sorts of issues and advantages typically come up too. Another aspect of flex-time worth considering, for instance, is that it evens out traffic and therefore cuts down on rush-hour traffic jams (which are also a cause of speeding since they slow people down and create impatience). Workplaces could encourage staggered schedules for this reason. Likewise, flex-time might cut down on the demand for new roads, which are typically designed with peak loads—rush-hour traffic—in mind, and therefore could save millions of dollars in construction and maintenance costs.

SUMMARY

The methods in this chapter ask you to rethink problems as they are usually presented. How can they be redefined? What are their causes? Are they necessarily even problems at all?

- *Think Laterally.* Survey all the outlying aspects of the problem in search of alternative approaches.
- *Find Opportunities in the Problem.* 'If life hands you a lemon, make lemonade!'
- *Try Prevention.* Ask how can this problem can be headed off before it even arises.

FOR PRACTICE

1. Use the tools introduced in this chapter to deal with the following list of everyday annoyances. In each case, ask yourself if there is a way to reframe 'the' problem—laterally, opportunistically, and/or proactively—*before* you consider how to 'solve' it.
    a) Habitual lateness: you or someone you depend on is repeatedly late for school or work.
    b) Loud neighbours: your neighbours (upstairs, downstairs, or next door) play loud music at unfortunate hours of the day or night.

c) Procrastination: you frequently put off your work until the last minute or until the deadline is past.

d) Long waits in line: all too often, you find yourself standing in line waiting (at the student loans office, the campus book store, the grocery store, the airport security checkpoint, etc.).

e) Weeds: was the American poet, essayist, and philosopher, Ralph Waldo Emerson right that a weed is just a plant we haven't yet figured out how to appreciate?

2. Here is a list of product-design issues to approach in the same way. Use all of the tools available, but especially those in this chapter.

a) Stuck cars: can you figure out ways to make cars better able to get themselves back on the road when they've slipped into a ditch or a snowbank? Can you figure out ways to avoid getting stuck in the first place?

b) Water heaters: most water heaters consume electricity or natural gases to keep large amounts of water heated even when we aren't using it. Can you think of more efficient and economical ways to heat water?

c) Green greens: automatic sprinkler systems used to maintain the fairways and greens at golf courses demand massive quantities of water. Can you think of a better way to maintain these courses without using so much water? Can you think of a better way to construct the courses so that less water is required?

d) Safe boating: personal watercraft or 'PWCS' (Jet Skis, Sea-Doos, etc.) are very fast. They are also small and relatively unstable compared with other boats. Indeed, it is common for drivers to fall off their PWCS when traveling at high speeds. To avoid having the PWC drive away on its own, current designs incorporate a tether that attaches to the driver's wrist. When the driver falls into the water, he or she becomes untethered and the PWC shuts off. Can you think of additional design elements that would make PWCS safer? Could these design elements be incorporated in other vehicles (snowmobiles, etc.)?

3. Here is a list of some major social problems. Identify the usual ways of approaching each problem and then work to reframe the problem using the tools introduced in this chapter.

   a) Homelessness: how did it come about that some people have no place to call home? Can you conceive of novel ways to address this issue?

   b) Suburban sprawl: does it create unique city-planning opportunities as well as problems?

   c) Obesity: can you think of alternatives to traditional binge-diets and exercise programs?

   d) Retirees: as an increasing number of the baby-boomer generation retires, a number of social issues arise. What might these retirees do with their time? How could society be restructured to respond to their needs and to better enable them to contribute?

   e) Performance-enhancing drug use: stories of athletes caught using performance-enhancing drugs are all over the media. Why do we think the use of performance-enhancing drugs is a problem? Are there ways to rethink this problem? Can you think of new ways of dealing with it?

   f) Jails: the penalty for most serious crimes is imprisonment. What other options might there be? How else might we approach the whole question of punishment and prison?

4. Use the methods introduced in this chapter to rethink the problems related to marriage. Here are two exercises to get started:

   a) Typically, only two 'answers' are presented to questions about the legal status of same-sex marriages: same-sex marriages should be allowed or they should not be allowed. Are there other, lateral, options?

   b) On the model that marriages are between one man and one woman, polygamous relationships are also ruled out. Use the methods presented in this book to rethink the problems related to polygamous relationships in North America. (For this, you might find the method of Compare and Contrast a good place to start.)

5. Too often, debates about important moral, social, and political issues are simplified to the point that the issues themselves become obscured. This happens, for instance, when the positions

of those involved in debates are simplified to the point that what critical thinkers call a false dichotomy or false dilemma is created. This is where an issue is presented in a manner suggesting there are only two positions to be defended and that participants in the debate must choose one or the other. Creative thinking can help us discern false dichotomies by helping us identify other possibilities. This is another way to start rethinking problems. The following exercises are about some well-known issues that tend to be oversimplified—'problems' that are in need of being rethought:

a) Science is often pitted against religion. This is seen, for example, in the characterization of debates about the origin of the universe and human beings. The scientific explanation, usually an evolution theory, is pitted against the religious explanation (for example, the Christian account known as Creationism). If we accept the scientific explanation, are we necessarily opposed to religion? If we accept religion are we necessarily opposed to science? How can we rethink this debate?

b) On November 6, 2001, in a news conference with French President, Jacques Chirac, American President George W. Bush asserted, 'You're either with us or against us in the fight against terror'. With this statement, Bush meant to put pressure on other countries to support the US-led attacks in Iraq. Consider whether Bush's statement represents the only possibilities. If not, what other possibilities are there?

c) Apply the tools introduced in this chapter to conceive of other ways to combat terrorism. (Notice, this exercise can be done *without* first thinking about the moral implications of the war in Iraq.)

d) These days, we see more public debate about the moral and legal status of abortion in the US than in Canada, though the issue is still a point of contention north of the border. In both countries, debates about abortion usually pit those who are 'pro-life' against those who are 'pro-choice'. Sometimes, people on the 'pro-choice' side of the debate are characterized as being 'for abortions' and people on the 'pro-life' side of the debate are characterized as failing to

CHAPTER SIX

FULL-TIME CREATIVITY

If you are intrigued by the possibilities for creative thinking introduced in the earlier chapters of this book, you might now turn your attention to other ways of incorporating creative thinking into your life. To give you a sense of the possibilities, this chapter paints a picture of creative thinking as a way of life.

CREATIVITY EVERY DAY

To feel the effects of thinking creatively, look around you, right now, wherever you are (maybe a schoolroom or library, maybe at home, maybe somewhere else). Take a good long look. Now ask yourself, 'How can this space be improved?' Are there one or two changes that you can make right now that would markedly improve the space? Why not make them? Even new lamps or new colours on the walls can make a difference in a room. Perhaps murals would be better. How about something as simple as opening the windows or rearranging the seating?

Anything is fair game. There are questions and possibilities every time you turn around. If you ride a bike, you might consider that uncomfortable little bike-helmet strap under your chin—there has got to be a better way. Figure it out. There are bumper-stickers on passing cars; could bikes have them too? (Where would they go? What shape would they have?) On a larger scale, how can your city be made more bikeable? (Are dedicated bike trails, or 'bike hours' when cars aren't allowed in certain lanes, possible?) Challenge yourself to generate additional solutions using the simple methods introduced in this book.

Maybe at a party you meet a person who leads dances for people with restricted mobility. He needs dances that people can do in wheelchairs or dances that are performed with the top halves of their bodies only. You could just smile and move on. You could also get creative right then and there. How about using some flags or streamers so that there is a dramatic sense of movement without great physical demands? Perhaps you could focus instead on finding (or inventing) a kind of dance that can *only* be done by people in wheelchairs.

Maybe creative thinking could help us find ways to remember our dreams better. What would it take? Perhaps some kind of training, or maybe a different way of waking up in the morning would work. Some people honour dreams as a source of divine inspiration, guidance, and affirmation. Even the great Greek philosopher Socrates trusted his dreams as a source of prophetic information. Could we imagine sharing our dreams with family and friends, rather than just keeping them to ourselves or sharing them with psychiatrists?

There is nothing mandatory about the way the world is right now. Everything is open to rethinking and change. Try to imagine how things could be, not just focus on how they are. The challenge is to do

CASE IN POINT

It is important to remember that finding a good solution often starts by getting clear on the problem itself. Significant controversy has surrounded the legal definition of 'marriage' recently. Of particular debate is whether same-sex unions can be recognized as marriages with all of the privileges and responsibilities that go along with this title. One aspect of the debate—and certainly there are others—concerns the fact that we are considering a definition. On the one hand, many traditionalists want to maintain that the definition of marriage means that a marriage can only be between one man and one woman. On the other hand, others argue that this begs an important question. The debate is about the legal definition of marriage, so appeal made to that definition is circular. In addition, some argue that marriage is defined within religious institutions and that most major religions do not recognize same-sex marriages (or are even opposed to same-sex relations) while others argue that the legal definition of marriage is separable from the religious conception of marriage.

Less than 100 years ago, the legal definition of 'persons' excluded women in Canada. This changed as the result of a campaign lead by women from Alberta: Emily Murphy, Henrietta Muir Edwards, Louise McKinney, Irene Parby, and Nellie McClung, now known as the *Famous Five* of women's suffrage. They challenged the courts, and in 1929 the Privy Council gave women legal status as persons. Strong opposition was encountered along the way.[1] Today, we think it obvious that women should be counted as persons under the law.

It is easy to see how these issues are related insofar as they both concern legal definitions that have the potential to exclude certain people from specific privileges and responsibilities. Without pushing any solution to the problem of defining marriage, thinking about these similarities helps us to understand one aspect of 'the' problem in a new light.

this *wherever* you are and *whenever* you can. Follow through by making some actual changes. Dream notebooks, new bike helmets (another business opportunity)—whatever it might be. You've already seen that you can make serious creative progress on everyday problems, from getting up in the morning to making better marriages. Full-time creative people make a regular practice of it. Sometimes they even get rich by it.

Besides, everyday creativity is also just plain fun. Coming up with new ideas is exciting even when they have no practical use whatsoever. That is why people like brain-teasers. Exotic association, brainstorming, mixing and matching, lateral thinking—this is not thinking-as-usual. There is a freshness and energy to it, and it adds a new spring to your step.

Creative thinking might just be healthy too. Scientists used to think that brain function gradually declines over one's whole life and that there is nothing much we can do about it. Now they think the opposite. Though some mental functions do gradually decline with time, others actually improve, at least until late old age; and—here's the key thing—almost all of them show less decline with more mental exercise.[2] Even though research hasn't yet established that the specific methods presented in this book increase our prospects for long-term mental health, there is every reason to think that we can increase our abilities as creative thinkers with practice.

What's more, when we use the various parts of our brains, circulation improves and new cells grow in. It's not enough to be physically active. You have to think hard too. It turns out that, like our bodies, our brains stay fit when exercised.

Creative Good Citizenship

Creative thinking is also a social contribution. And it is not just that occasionally you may save a drowning swimmer or re-energize a boring weather report. Think again of the many social problems we have tackled. Maybe by now you have found a completely new way of thinking about drugs, travel, school, TV programming, recycling, and so on. With the simple methods in this book, you are equipped to find many more. Creative thinking along these lines can improve life for all of us.

CASE IN POINT

Significant changes often start with a single act. Jack Miner, of Kingsville, Ontario, was curious to know where the ducks that spent their summers on his farm went in the winter. He scratched his address on a bit of scrap metal and bent this around the leg of a mallard, hoping that someone would inform him if the duck was found in the winter. This was in 1909. Unfortunately for the duck, it was shot in the early months of 1910. Fortunately for us, the bit of metal was returned to Miner by the hunter in South Carolina who had shot the duck. We now know quite a lot about the migratory habits of birds, and much of this comes from the practice of 'banding' or 'tagging'—that is, from the simple practice of scratching some information on a band or tag attached to the bird and having that information relayed back to the source each time the bird is encountered. Fortunately, these practices no longer rely on the destruction of the birds to collect the information.[3]

Social creativity has its full-time requirements too. Practice creativity as visibly, explicitly, and invitingly as you can. This can draw in other people. Teach it to your children when or if you have any. Talk to people—to family, to friends, to students, to teachers, to co-workers, to colleagues, and to elected officials. Talk to anyone who will talk about new ideas. The 'idea person' in an organization or on the block is the one who steps up to creativity. You've got the tools, why can't it be you?

With the best of your new ideas, go public. Write letters to the editor of your local newspaper. Make constructive suggestions rather than complaining or criticizing. Most newspapers are happy to consider guest editorials—check your local paper's website for a link to the editorial page. People have even organized problem-solving shows on local radio stations. Callers phone in their problems, and the hosts brainstorm right on the air.

Go to meetings of your Student Council or Cabinet, City Council, and similar organizations. You might be surprised at how few other people show up on a regular basis. Just one person willing to speak up often can make a real difference. Don't hesitate to contact your representatives or other decision-makers (school principals, university presidents, employers, council and government representatives, etc.) either. Get some new ideas into circulation.

Much of this may sound familiar. Really it's just plain old good citizenship with a creative edge.

Every so often you will run up against an Eeyore who dismisses your ideas as too radical or impossible, no matter how promising they appear to you. In this event, combine your creative ideas with the tools of critical thinking. Generate compelling arguments to convince the naysayers that the changes you propose are both possible and worthwhile.

Luckily, most people are open to new ideas. Most of the time you will encounter an aspect of good citizenship that is not so familiar: the power of creative thinking to inspire people. It's not very often that employers, say, or elected representatives hear from people with creative suggestions. Most people either just gripe or advocate some prepackaged position—and the vast majority never take part at all. But

CASE IN POINT

There are global organizations seeking out and featuring new ideas for bettering the world. One of these is the Institute for Social Inventions, a British organization that runs a global website called the *Global Ideas Bank* and publishes collections of great ideas every few years with inspiring titles like *The Book of Visions* and *Setting the World Alight*.

Visit their website (www.globalideasbank.org) for literally thousands of great ideas and for links to other web resources.

On the website, the *Global Ideas Bank* defines a 'social invention' as 'a new or imaginative way of tackling a social problem or improving the quality of life', something that 'changes the way in which people relate to themselves or each other, either individually . . . or collectively'. On the website you'll find ideas about teaching music to the (supposedly) 'unmusical', self-constructed housing for the homeless, new kinds of childbirth, alternative forms of extended care for the elderly (including new ideas about dying well), taxing TV violence, and all sorts of other issues. Some of the ideas about marriage and naming introduced in Chapter 4 of this book are also found there.

Anyone can submit an idea to the *Global Ideas Bank*. Submissions are screened by the editors for originality and appropriateness; so only the best make it to the books. There are even cash prizes for the year's best ideas. (Note that *The Body Shop* has a similar prize—in fact, they have a whole department of social innovation, as do many companies and workplaces: there are even jobs in this field!)

we're all drawn to new ideas, to the sense that even really tough problems have hopeful possibilities. And, most basically, people are drawn to the creative spirit that shows itself when a person starts to look for new ideas. Anyone whose attitude is creative and promising will stand out—and then your ideas can go a long way.

Creativity To Change The World

Radical creativity can also change the world. Radical changes can result from creative thinking on a large scale.[4] When thinking creatively, our challenge is not to shrink from even the wildest and most utopian hopes.

Take the car, for example. In the last century, we have gone from a few curiosities putt-putting harmlessly around the back roads to 600 million–plus cars on the planet, clogging up city streets, ruling economies, and even altering the climate. It is easy to despair over these truly massive problems. But the very fact that the car has become so dominant so quickly could also be read the other way around: as an encouragement to visualize the next big change. If such an absolutely dramatic change was possible in only a century (mostly in the last half-century, really), then other dramatic changes are almost certainly possible. It's up to us to imagine what's next.

Already cars are being remade before our eyes. In 1972, the Canadian Ministry of Transport along with a number of US organizations hosted a competition to develop energy-efficient cars that produce little or no pollution. Two Canadian entries, one from a team of students at the University of British Columbia and another from a team of students at the University of Western Ontario and Fanshawe College took away top prizes. The entry from UBC, which took away the highest overall award, included a number of features that are becoming standard on the cars produced by major automotive manufacturers today. They include instruments displaying tire pressure and other details relevant to smooth running. Project-cars like these have been instrumental in the development and testing of new fuels, better electric motors, more efficient and affordable batteries, and many other innovations that we now find in mass-produced automobiles. Students can and do make a difference with their creativity.

Since 1987, the *World Solar Challenge* has been hosted in Australia. This event originally pitted solar-power cars in a race against each other across the Australian outback. The cars, designed by professional and student engineers from around the world, are now capable of speeds beyond those allowed by Australian law. Thus, it has been decided to change the challenge from an all-out race to the development of cars that could, with little change, be produced for everyday consumption and use. Perhaps among the new rules should be a limit on the top speed of the entries—this would incorporate a ridiculously simple solution to the problem of speeding introduced in Chapter 5 too—cars that cannot break the speed limit will not break the speed limit.

Many creative innovations are already on our roads. Conversion kits are available to retrofit diesel engines so they run on nothing but used cooking oil—a low-emissions, recycled fuel that carries the faint, but not always unwelcome, smell of whatever the oil was used to cook. Hybrid engines radically improve mileage; fuel-cell and hydrogen engines offer enormously improved efficiency and no emissions except water.

In the wake of the global economic meltdown in 2008 and 2009, the 'Big 3' automotive manufacturers in North America have been working to reinvent themselves. As a result, a good deal more attention is being paid to the sorts of products being offered. Perhaps a new generation of technology will soon be on our roads.

Better cars, though, are really only a temporary, or limited, solution. Death and mayhem on the roads, traffic jams, highway costs and land loss, political and environmental harms—most of these problems would remain.

Alternatives to cars are on the way. South American and European cities are already limiting cars or banning them entirely, and have built sparkling and efficient public bus or train systems with the savings from not having to pay for so many roads, wrecks, parking ramps, traffic cops, etc. Urban planners design high-density developments around new transit stops so that people can get from home to work, stores, schools, and other destinations with only a short walk from each stop.

These are positive solutions, but we can go farther. What about 'bike buses', say, that pick up bike riders from gathering spots, quickly transport them ten or twenty miles over high-speed tracks or roads, and then drop them off so they can efficiently disperse to wherever they are going? These services are already popular in Ottawa, Toronto, Edmonton, Kingston, Thunder Bay, Vancouver, Williams Lake, Whitehorse, and other cities across the country. What else can you think of? Perhaps there are better ways to organize carpools or ways to promote safe hitchhiking. What about new kinds of rickshaws?

But we still have not gotten as radical as we might. Suppose now that we go back to the very beginning and frame 'the' problem in a different way. Rather than providing better cars or even better public transit, wouldn't it make more sense to reduce or eliminate the need for commutes in the first place? Suppose people could stay home or in the neighbourhood most of the time. Shopping could be local again, as it was not so long ago, with corner groceries and farmer's markets complemented by the latest forms of Internet shopping for less commonly sought and durable goods. We could telecommute, shifting many jobs to local community centres like high-tech branch libraries or a neighbourhood Internet café plus childcare centres, schools, and gardens. (Sweden is already building such 'tele-cottages' nationwide.) We could promote 'virtual travel', maybe, and when we take actual, physical vacation trips, we could take them long and slow: walk, bike, ride a horse, ride a camel. . . . Doesn't that sound like a better life?

Here are a few more radical ideas.

We have come to recognize that we are all citizens of one Earth. Yet our politics are driven by national rivalries. If we are to have a truly global politics, must it be built on top of the nation-states? Maybe we should not think about global order on the model of a government at all but on something like a network—a rich set of interconnections, contacts, and dialogues. And if that sounds familiar, it should. Could it be that an entirely new form of direct global politics is now possible through the Internet? Why are we not already e-mailing directly with Iraqis, Israelis, South Africans? (Perhaps, in your own social networking, you already do?) How much would it take to create systematic, large-scale contacts of this sort? What might evolve from them? New kinds of global representatives, spokespeople, leaders?

Then there is the question of space travel. When humans finally take off for Mars, are they going to be the familiar all-human round-trip crew piloting a capsule and driven by burning Earth's fossil fuels? It's almost inconceivable, actually: without radical new technologies, we can't send enough air, food, or fuel to last the whole trip. What then? Might we have to rethink what space missions are, who goes on them—in fact, *everything* about them?

For starters, why not one-way trips? Could we find extraordinary people, maybe more the adventurer and the poet types, who'd be willing to ship out for good? It's a lot easier to drop people on planets than to get them back off.

The question of life-support requires some rethinking too. Perhaps a whole community of plants and animals should go to replenish the air and provide food for each other and for the humans: a sort of Earth-in-miniature. How would such a craft look? How shall we think of it: more like an ark, maybe, than a capsule?

And what drives an ark? We are at the point of testing space probes that ride the solar winds: sailboats, in effect, to the stars. Others envision living forms—spacecraft grown rather than made, with trees bio-engineered inside-out (as epic poet and science fiction writer Frederick Turner imagines them, with a huge sealed central shaft sunlighting the forests and fields growing within.[5]

And why not send life back out into the cosmos, even creating Earth-like atmospheres elsewhere, on Mars for example, which we know has enough gravity, an atmosphere, and some evidence of water?

SUMMARY

This chapter encourages you to make creative thinking a regular part of your life. This is not hard to do, though it will take some practice before it becomes habit. Remember:

- *Nothing is off-limits.* Use the methods in this book to look for new solutions to everyday problems and to identify areas in our lives that could be improved even if we don't (yet) identify them as problems.
- *Rethink 'the' problem.* In every case, remember to rethink the problem as a starting point. Clarifying a problem goes a long way toward finding solutions.
- *Challenge yourself.* Use the tools of creative thinking when you are stuck with a problem or, better, whenever you have the chance.
- *Act on your ideas.* Even the best ideas remain ideas alone until we act on them. If you have a good idea, act on it. Put it into practice, post it to the Global Ideas Bank, apply for a patent, or whatever. Good ideas can change the world for the better when we act on them.

But enough of these. These are sweeping and sketchy ideas about very large issues. They are certainly not the only ideas or necessarily the best ideas. In the end, they might not even be good ideas. The main point is only that new and radically creative ideas are possible. And again, they must come from somewhere—why not us? If these are not to your taste—or even if they are—you know what to do. . . .

FOR PRACTICE

1. This chapter encourages you to make creative thinking a regular feature of the way you identify and respond to problems in your life. This starts with noticing what needs change. The following exercises will help you start paying attention to opportunities for applying your creativity.

   a) Make a list of twenty things that need change. Start with what is right next to you and gradually move your focus toward the larger world. (Some of what you notice may suggest personal changes, some may open business opportunities, some may launch political campaigns, and so on.)

   b) Use the methods from this book to add to the list you've generated in 1a).

   c) Pick one thing in need of change from your list. Clarify the problem: why does that thing need change?

   d) Apply the methods from this book to reframe the problem identified in 1c) and to start generating possible solutions.

   e) Is it possible to implement the solutions outlined in 1d)? (If so, why not do it?)

2. Humans have a knack for creating problems. Consider the following questions to identify creative opportunities in some of these problems.

   a) Are there positive ways to address the destructive impact we are having on natural environments? What, exactly, is the root of our environmental issues? Are there ways to recast these issues in a new light (you might consider that we tend to focus on dangers and disasters)?

b) Attending university or college is not cheap. Currently, students can apply for grants and loans, though many students end up carrying a part-time or full-time job all year in order to pay for their education. Clarify the problem or problems related to the costs of education. Are there ways to rethink the problem(s)? Can you think of alternative models for funding university and college education?

c) North Americans worry about losing manufacturing jobs to cheaper (perhaps exploitative) foreign factories. At the same time, we negotiate the highest possible wages for ourselves and insist on the lowest possible prices on the goods we purchase. Can you envision a system that promotes job security, high wages, and inexpensive products? Or, more generally, can you conceive of better economic models than what we have now?

d) Armies are good for fighting wars. In recent history, armies have been used for peacekeeping and for helping to (re) build functioning societies. The ongoing Canadian mission in Afghanistan is an example of attempts to use armies for functions other than fighting wars. It remains an open question whether armies can establish peace or functioning societies. So far the evidence suggests there must be better ways to perform these functions. Can you envision a better way to establish peace in war-torn areas of the world? Can you envision a better way to help (re)build functioning societies?

3. The text box on the definition of marriage invites you to rethink the debate about the legal status of same-sex unions by considering one similarity it shares with the historical debate about the legal status of women: both concern legal definitions. Given this similarity, we might be tempted to generate what critical thinkers call an argument by analogy. We might come to the conclusion that we should alter the legal definition of marriage to recognize same-sex marriages. The argument might go something like this: *The debate about the legal status of same-sex unions is analogous to the debate about the legal status of women as persons.*

Both are concerned with whether to expand legal definitions to be more inclusive. Since we think it was right to expand the legal definition of persons to include women, it would be right to expand the legal definition of marriage to include same-sex unions. Is the similarity identified enough to make this a compelling argument? To answer this question, use the methods introduced in this book to identify additional points of analogy or disanalogy that are relevant.

4. Challenge yourself to define problems related to each of the following topics. Apply the tools from this book to start working on these problems creatively.
   a) Health care
   b) National security
   c) Community
   d) Aging
   e) Pollution
   f) Population
   g) Child care
   h) Education
   i) The global economy
   j) Poverty

There are many extended introductions to creative thinking. Most of these are written for an audience interested in business. The list of such texts includes Edward de Bono, *Serious Creativity* (HarperCollins, 1992) and *Lateral Thinking* (Harper, 1970); Barry Nalebuff and Ian Ayres, *Why Not? How to Use Everyday Ingenuity to Solve Problems Big and Small* (Harvard Business School Press, 2003); Charlie and Maria Girsch, *Inventivity* (Creativity Central, 1999); and Marvin Levine, *Effective Problem-Solving* (Prentice Hall, second edition, 1993). On proactive thinking, Stephen Covey's *The Seven Habits of Highly Effective People* (Simon and Schuster, 1990) is a classic.

For the application of creativity to problems in ethics, see also Anthony Weston's *Creative Problem-Solving in Ethics* (Oxford University Press, 2007). *Creative Problem-Solving in Ethics* is aimed at doing for students interested in ethics what *Creativity for Critical Thinkers* does for students interested in critical thinking. Most of the methods and themes are similar, but the applications and examples differ.

Chapter 1:

1. Variations of 'At the Bus Stop' are widely circulated by email. The specific origin of the story presented is unknown.
2. This problem is adapted from an example in Bill Mollison, *Permaculture* (Tagari, 1988).
3. Edward De Bono, *Lateral Thinking* (Harper, 1970).
4. For more information on the 'vision' behind Erickson's design, see the University of Lethbridge's website: www.uleth.ca/exp/vision/.

Chapter 2:

1. Ronald Melzack, 'The Tragedy of Needless Pain', *Scientific American*, 262, 2 (1990): 27–33.
2. For a review of research related to 'inattention blindness', see: Daniel J. Simons and Christopher F. Chabris, 'Gorillas in our midst: sustained inattentional blindness for dynamic events', *Perception*, 28 (1999): 1059–74 and Daniel J. Simons, 'Attentional capture and inattentional blindness', *Trends Cogn Sci.*, 4, 4 (2000): 147–55.
3. For more information, see Amos Tversky and Daniel Kahneman, 'Extension versus intuitive reasoning: The conjunction fallacy in probability judgment', *Psychological Review*, 90, 4 (1983): 293–315 and 'Judgments of and by representativeness', in Daniel Kahneman, Paul Slovic, and Amos Tversky (eds.), *Judgment under uncertainty: Heuristics and biases* (Cambridge University Press, 1982).
4. Simone Sandkuhler and Joydeep Bhattacharya, 'Deconstructing Insight: EEG Correlates of Insightful Problem Solving', *PLoS ONE*,

3, 1 (2008) available at: www.plosone.org/article/info:doi/10.1371/journal.pone.0001459.

5. Something like the random-word method appears in nearly every creativity text including those cited above. This method has been expanded here to include other kinds of exotic association.

6. John Bankston, *Alexander Fleming and the Story of Penicillin* (Mitchell Lane Publishers, 2002).

7. *Canadian Intellectual Property Office* webpage: www.cipo.ic.gc.ca/eic/site/cipointernet-internetopic.nsf/eng/wr00930.html.

8. *National Research Council* webpage: www.nrc-cnrc.gc.ca/eng/news/nrc/2003/06/02/hopps.html.

9. Walter Gratzer, *Eurekas and Euphorias: The Oxford Book of Scientific Anecdotes* (Oxford University Press, 2002). For an account of the status of this, and other, stories surrounding Kekulé's 'discovery', see: John H. Wotiz, *The Kekulé Riddle: A challenge for chemists and psychologists* (Cache River Press, 1993).

Chapter 3:

1. Variations on the methods developed here are common in the books listed in the 'Further Reading' section above.

2. Alex F. Osborn, *Applied imagination: principles and procedures of creative problem-solving,* 3rd Ed. (Charles Scribner's Sons, 1979), p. 151. The first edition of this book was published in 1953. By then "brainstorming" was more than a decade old.

3. Ibid. p. 156.

4. Edward de Bono, *Serious Creativity* (HarperCollins, 1992).

5. Reva Seth, *First Comes Marriage: Modern Relationship Advice from the Wisdom of Arranged Marriages* (Simon and Schuster, 2008).

6. Albrecht Folsing, (trans. Ewald Osers), *Albert Einstein: A Biography* (Penguin Books, 1998).

7. For more information, see www.playpumps.org. The story of the Play Pump, 'South Africa: The Play Pump: Turning water into child's play' by Jackie Bennion was released online by www.pbs.org/frontlineworld/ on October 24, 2005. See www.pbs.org/frontlineworld/rough/2005/10/south_africa_th.html.

8. 'The Slick-Licker' *Time*, Monday, October 25, 1971. Article available at: www.time.com/time/magazine/article/0,9171,877344,00. html.

9. The story of the G-suit is told in: Michael Bliss, *Banting: A Biography* (University of Toronto Press, 1991), p. 255. (Franks was Banting's colleague.)

10. Ralph Nader, Nadia Milleron, and Duff Conacher, *Canada Firsts* (McClelland & Stewart Inc., 1992), p. 26.

Chapter 4:

1. Barry Nalebuff and Ian Ayres, *Why Not? How to Use Everyday Ingenuity to Solve Problems Big and Small* (Harvard Business School Press, 2003).

2. Roderick Phillips, *Untying the Knot: A Short History of Divorce* (Cambridge University Press, 1991).

3. The two extended ideas with which this chapter ends can also be found on the *Global Ideas Bank* website: www. globalideasbank. org. See, 'Couples for Community' by Ashlee Finecey and 'Couples Choose New Middle Name' by Anthony Weston. Weston's idea is also published as 'Beyond Hyphenation: A New System for Nonsexist Family Names', *CoEvolution Quarterly* 41, 1 (1984): 30–33.

4. 'Pioneer for Women's Equality Remembered' by Jason Unrau, *Whitehorse Daily Star*, March 11, 2009. This article is available at: http://whitehorsestar.com/archive/story/pioneer-for-womens-equality-remembered/. See also the *Government of Yukon* website news release ('Women's History Month Poster Celebrates Yukon's Women's Mini-Bus Society', October 16, 2008) available at: www. gov.yk.ca/news/2008/08-249.html.

5. *Iceland Ministry of Justice and Ecclesiastical Affairs* webpage: http://eng.domsmalaraduneyti.is/information/nr/125.

6. *Service Alberta* webpage: www.servicealberta.ca/790.cfm.

7. *Government of Quebec* webpage: www.justice.gouv.qc.ca/english/publications/generale/maria-a.htm.

8. 'Married name dilemma: his or hers?' *Montreal Gazette*, Friday, November 30, 2007.

9. 'How they let the GoodTimes roll', *thestar.com*, Saturday, May 30, 2009. Article available at: www.thestar.com/living/article/640836.

10. The statistic presented here is supported by a survey conducted by the *Center For Survey Research* at Indiana University. The results were presented as 'Constructing the Family in the 21st Century' on Tuesday, August 11, 2009 at the Annual Meeting of the American Sociological Association. Another survey, conducted in 2008 by Harris Interactive for *The Knot Wedding Network*, www.theknot. com, puts the number at 88 per cent.

Chapter 5:

1. The origin of this story is unknown, though it closely resembles an actual event involving a man saving another man's life using a hose from a vacuum cleaner as a snorkel. For this, see, 'Vacuum cleaner hose saves trapped worker in Mordialloc Creek accident' by Anthony Dowsley, www.news.com.au/heraldsun/, June 1, 2009, 5:07 p.m. It is also central to Andre Dubus' 'The Doctor', *The New Yorker*, April 26, 1969 in which the main character sees a child held underwater by a concrete slab. He can't find help at a nearby house and spends his efforts trying to move the concrete slab off of the boy who eventually drowns. Days later, the doctor realizes that he could have saved the boy with a makeshift snorkel.

2. The story of Archimedes is preserved in Vitruvius' *De Architectura*, Book IX, 9–12.

3. For more information about Canada's contribution to the *Phoenix* mission (launched in 2007), see: www.asc-csa.gc.ca/eng/astronomy/phoenix/default.asp.

4. For more information about NASA's Mars Rovers, see http://marsrovers.nasa.gov/home/index.html.

5. Holly C. Hanrahan, David A. Minton, Fred R. DeJarnett, Ivan A. Camelier, and Michael H. Fleming. 'Conceptual Designs for a Mars Tumbleweed'. *Proc. Int. Workshop 'Planetary Probe Atmospheric Entry and Descent Trajectory Analysis and Science'*. Lisbon, Portugal, 6–9 October 2003. Also published as: ESA *SP-544*, (2004): 339–42.

6. *Inventive Women* website: www.inventivewomen.com.

7. Ibid.

8. Historical information about Buckley's advertising strategies is available on their website: www.buckleys.com/about/index.htm.

9. Historical information about Frontier College is available on the organization's website: www.frontiercollege.ca.

10. On viewing wastes as resources, see Paul Hawken, Amory Lovins, and L. Hunter Lovins, *Natural Capitalism* (Little, Brown, 1999).

11. Jane Brody, 'TV's Toll on Young Minds and Bodies', *New York Times*, August 3, 2004, p. D7.

Chapter 6:

1. 'Alberta Online Encyclopaedia' at: www.abheritage.ca/famous5/educational/nation_builders.html.

2. The *Baycrest Research Centre for Aging and the Brain*, along with the *Rotman Research Institute* and the *Kunin-Lunenfild Applied Research Unit* in Toronto supports research in this area. For some of their results and references to specific academic articles, see the *Baycrest* webpage: www.baycrest.org/Research.

3. Ralph Nader, Nadia Milleron, and Duff Conacher, *Canada Firsts* (McClelland & Stewart Inc., 1992), pp. 97–8.

4. In addition to the Hawkins and Lovins book cited in Chapter 5 (note 10), two other books of radical change ideas are Bruce Mau and Jennifer Leonard, *Massive Change* (Phaidon, 2004), and David Bornstein, *How to Change the World: Social Entrepreneurs and the Power of New Ideas* (Oxford University Press, 2004).

5. Frederick Turner's vision of living space vessels is drawn from his masterful and suggestive epic poem, *Genesis* (Saybrook Publishing, 1988).